just the
two of us

First published 2003 by Contender Books
Contender Books is a division of
The Contender Entertainment Group
48 Margaret Street
London
W1W 8SE

This edition published 2003

1 3 5 7 9 10 8 6 4 2

ISBN 1 84357 092 0

Printed in the UK by Butler & Tanner Ltd, Frome and London
Cover and text design by Button One-to-One
Typesetting by E-Type
Edited by Emily Gale
Production by Sasha Morton

Plate section photographs supplied by Fiona Inglis, Camera Press and
Maya Salinger / Ilka Peemoeller.

just the
two of us

Fiona Inglis

contents

acknowledgements

To my son, without his support this book wouldn't have been possible. I am very, very proud of what you have achieved and love you so much.

Thank you so much to Tessa, who has been so incredibly supportive and enthusiastic with her advice on bringing my story to life.

And to all the staff at Contender Books, who have been extremely friendly and encouraging with this, my first book – a project which I never imagined possible.

This book is dedicated to my mother and father.

chapter one

The Two of Us

Outside the lights and street scenes of late-night London slid past. Inside I sank back into the wonderfully cocooning luxury of the chauffeur-driven limo, sipped champagne and revelled in the moment. I had woken early on that morning of 20 February, my birthday, to a pleasant feeling of inner happiness and a strange certainty that today was going to bring great things. My son Duncan and all the boys in Blue had been nominated for Best British Newcomers at pop's most glittering awards ceremony, The BRITs. Beside me was my friend, Andrea Costa, Antony's mum, and we were heading for the VIP after-show party.

My mobile bleeped and I heard Duncan on the line trying to tell me something, but high buildings made the reception terrible and all I could hear were disjointed words before we were cut off completely. Minutes before we arrived at the nightclub he rang again. Suddenly the message was loud and clear: 'Mum, we've won! We've won!'

Andrea and I were still clutching each other's arms and half-laughing, half-crying as we arrived minutes later at the party held at a nightclub called The Collection in Knightsbridge. The doorman sprang forward to open the car door and we entered down a spectacular long glass bridge lit with candles and coloured lights. Suddenly Duncan was grabbing me in a bear hug and I was hugging him back and feeling overwhelmed with a fierce flood of pride mixed with other, less tangible, emotions that made speech impossible. It was all so very far away from that day 22 years ago when I had held a tiny baby in my arms and felt terribly, frighteningly alone.

*   *   *

The year was 1979 and I was experiencing a rather different car journey. I was wearing a Dorothy Perkins nightdress and dressing-gown and half-sitting, half-lying, in the back of a Vauxhall VX490 saloon, clutching the edge of the seat and groaning as waves of pain coursed through me. At the wheel, as we rattled through the empty Dorset roads in the small hours of that April morning, was not my husband or even a boyfriend. Instead, ramrod straight as befitted a retired army colonel, and driving as fast as he dared, was my 60-year-old father. Next to him, turning round anxiously with words of encouragement which I neither heard nor heeded, was my white-haired mum. As the pain mounted and my groans turned to shrieks, she gripped her handbag more nervously. Unbeknown to me it contained a pair of kitchen scissors which she had stuffed in at the last minute, should the worst come to the worst and they find themselves having to cut the umbilical cord in an emergency roadside delivery.

I was about to give birth to a baby whose father had not only broken off our engagement when I became pregnant, but had unceremoniously dumped me on my parents' doorstep, refused to acknowledge any responsibility for our child and ignored all my letters. It was a million miles from the future my parents had imagined for their only daughter. It was a million miles from the future I had imagined for myself.

The day before I had gone for a regular check-up with our family doctor, a lovely woman called Dr Joan. She felt my tummy to establish the baby's position and said, 'I think you've got about another ten days to go, dear.' That night I woke at one o'clock in the morning to an alarming sensation of dampness in the bed and an agonising low back ache. I sat up, prompting another flood, and realised that my waters had broken while I was asleep. In a panic I shouted for my mother who was immediately thrown into a similar state, dashing back on to the landing saying, 'I'll have to wake your father!' I was very frightened and in truth I think my mother was too, but my father was not to be rattled. His first reaction was that it was almost certainly a false alarm and I heard him saying as much to my mother, adding: 'Go back to sleep, woman.'

With the instinctive certainty that overtakes a woman in labour, however, I knew differently. This baby was going to be born, and soon. I knew I had to get to the hospital. In response to my urgent insistence and now occasional groans as the contractions began to grip, my father got up and soon had the motor running. It was only 22 miles from our home in Blandford, Dorset, to Oddstock Hospital in Salisbury, but it seemed like two hundred more. The car was so full of emotion. The fear and nervousness I felt about the birth began to mount and, even as the pain drove most thoughts from my mind, I was aware of a terrible sense of isolation. I was going through one of the most powerful and intimate experiences of a woman's life and I had no one to share it with. My parents, so wonderfully supportive in every way, must also have been gripped by an equally potent cocktail of sadness, anxiety and frustration at the role they had been forced into.

'How much further, how much further?' I pleaded in the brief seconds between the increasingly frequent contractions. There were no speed bumps in those days to impede our progress down the road to the hospital and we screeched to a halt outside the maternity block. Nurses responded to my parents' agitated state and I was taken directly to the delivery room. By now it was 2.30am and the doctor who examined me said it was too late for Pethidine as I was about to go into the second stage of labour.

The next couple of hours are a bit of a blur, overshadowed by horrific pain. The nurse offered me gas and air but for some insane reason I refused. I was fighting every contraction and somehow felt it might make me lose control. Instead, when the pains came, I hung on to the bars of the hospital bedstead. Sweat trickled down my forehead into my eyes and shyly I asked the nurse to wipe my brow. I sensed my request had annoyed her. The nurses were strict and stern, not warm or encouraging, but I wasn't afraid of their detached, clinical attitude because I had spent years boarding at a convent. It was what I was used to. Outside the delivery room my parents waited anxiously. Although I felt so alone, the idea of having my mother there was even worse. We were both much too inhibited; it would have been too embarrassing, despite the excruciating pain.

Soon they were telling me to push. There was an intense burning sensation and then all of a sudden my baby just shot out. The time was 4.55am and he weighed 8lb 5oz. The whole labour had taken less than four hours, which for a first baby was extraordinarily quick. Unfortunately a side effect of his rapid arrival into the world and his healthy weight was that I tore very badly, though I wasn't aware of that at the time.

When the nurses handed me my baby my first thought was, 'He's got really squashed eyes.' I was in something of a state of shock and I chose to focus on the insignificant detail of his puffy eyelids, caused by his dramatic entrance into the world, to block out the bigger emotions that might overwhelm me. It was all so very strange. One minute you're not a mother, the next you are and you've got this little tiny creature who is going to depend on you for every single thing. And for me there was something even more strange to deal with. Something which, gradually, in that small bare hospital room, I allowed to seep through into my consciousness: this was the first time in my life I had held, touched or even met another person who was my own flesh and blood. I had been adopted as a baby by my loving parents, who that night were still waiting anxiously outside the delivery room, and this was my only encounter with someone who was physically related to me.

I held that little mite, wrapped in his cotton NHS blanket, very tightly. He stared back with bright dark eyes that, beneath the swollen lids, suddenly seemed so full of ancient wisdom.

'It's just the two of us,' I told him, and felt excitement, happiness and also a strange pain as I planted a kiss on his tiny forehead.

chapter two

Secrets

Our garage was made of grapes, which hung down in lush green bunches over the roof of our yellow Vauxhall Victor car. When you looked up at the green ceiling of vine leaves you could see the sun flickering through. We were living in Cyprus, where my father was posted with the army, and one of my earliest memories is my father carrying me on his shoulders out to the garage and me reaching up to pinch a fat, ripe grape to eat. Another vivid memory from that time is of crawling on my hands and knees and putting my face to the cats' bowl to eat their food and, on another occasion, toddling in my nappy down a dirt path with a centipede in my hand. What especially sticks in my mind is my father's alarmed reaction as he jumped forward to knock the insect out of my grasp and flick it away.

I had an idyllic childhood. It was a lovely, carefree time and I was very lucky. I had an older brother, Alistair, two years ahead of me and later a younger brother, Roddy, arrived, who was three years younger. We were all adopted and all came from different families.

My father, Donald, was a highly intelligent and thoughtful man. His natural inclination was to help people and he believed very much that there was a proper code of behaviour, a decent way to behave. He had been an only child and spent much of his school years in Portsmouth, where his father was based in the Navy. As a boy he suffered from polio and at one time he was in a wheelchair with gloomy predictions about whether he would be able to walk again. Fortunately he made a full recovery. Later the family moved back up to Grimsby in Lincolnshire, where they came from originally. Although both his parents were Anglican, at the age of 17 my father converted to Catholicism. To this day I don't know what lay behind his decision, but a few years later his parents followed their son's example.

He wanted to be a doctor and was accepted at medical college, but during the second year he faced another serious health setback. He began to suffer frequent and increasingly severe headaches and after rounds of tests he was diagnosed as having a brain tumour. His parents were desperate to get the best treatment for their son and had heard of pioneering work in London by a neurosurgeon who'd realised that the care patients received after brain surgery was critical to their survival. This, remember, was towards the end of the 1930s when high-tech intensive care units as we have now were unimaginable. To focus on nursing and aftercare was a radical idea. The surgeon believed it was critical that patients retained consciousness once they came round from the anaesthetic and were not allowed to risk slipping into coma. Fortunately the brain tumour proved to be benign. My father's vivid memories from this time were of the nurses repeatedly slapping his face to keep him awake.

His parents' determination to get him the best care had paid off and once more he made a full recovery, but it destroyed his ambitions of becoming a doctor. He turned instead to his second choice, the Army. But before he signed up for what was to prove a highly successful career, he met and fell in love with my mother.

While his commitment to the Catholic faith may have brought him comfort during the dark days in hospital, it also provided an unexpected direction to his personal life. It was at the local Catholic church that he first met my mother, Kathleen, in 1941. He was 19, she was 21, and within a short time they were engaged, but war temporarily intervened in their plans to marry. My mother was trained as a secretary and worked in a civilian capacity for the Intelligence Services during the war, while my father joined the Signals Regiment and was distinguished as the youngest ever commissioned officer. They eventually married in 1942 in what my mother captioned in family photo albums as 'our hurried wedding'.

By the time I arrived my mother was in her early forties and they had already adopted Alistair, presumably after they had spent years trying unsuccessfully to have their own family. It was not until later that my curiosity was to lead me to discover why that time in Cyprus, where my earliest memories are set, was especially poignant for my parents. As a toddler I had no awareness of anything but the happiest of times spent playing in our beautiful, sunny garden. We stayed there for two and a half years and my world revolved around my mother and my older brother Alistair. He and I played endless games with a Robin Hood and Maid Marion theme. He would pretend to shoot me and then also have to come to my rescue, carrying me off in his arms. I did everything he said and was thrilled to be part of his exciting, imaginary life. Those years spent in a warm climate also meant we learned to swim very early. My mother, who was an excellent swimmer herself, used to take us to a swimming pool nearby and we grew up confident and at home in the water.

Just before we returned to England, the third member of our family joined us. My younger brother Roddy was born in Cyprus and my parents brought him back with them as a young baby to our next home, which was in Cardiff. Like Alistair and I, he was adopted and later I was to realise there was a special reason behind my parents' desire to add a third baby to their family. At the time, however, Roddy was simply an adorable baby I could cuddle and push about in his pram.

Roddy's arrival meant Alistair and I had to share a bedroom in our new house. I was four years old and my memory of this home, which like all our others was rented, was having to drive under an archway into a square with all the houses set around a grassy centre. I didn't mind sharing a bedroom, in fact it was rather fun. At night, after we had been put to bed, we used to get up and creep down to the kitchen to make a sickly concoction of cocoa powder, sugar and water mixed into a paste in an eggcup. We were obsessed with cocoa. My mother had another, altogether healthier, habit regarding food that dates from this time. After we were asleep she would creep in to check on us and put a piece of fruit on a plate on the little table by my bed. I didn't necessarily eat it, but it was something that I loved seeing when I woke up, whether it was an apple or an orange. It was her little surprise for me every morning.

My father was away a lot, either working long hours or sometimes going abroad. When he came back from such trips he'd bring me a doll in the national costume of the country and soon I had quite a collection. He was a glamorous, dashing figure, very tall and slim in his uniform, and when he was home there was always music in the house. He was a very good pianist and sitting down to play was his relaxation. I grew up with music and there was always a piano in the house. He liked classical music but he also played songs like 'Stormy Weather' and 'The Way You Look Tonight'. He often used to sing the latter song slightly teasingly to my mother, while she was engrossed in one of the 'whodunnit' books she loved to get from the library. She would look embarrassed and tell him to stop but he would just smile and sing on; he adored her.

From the earliest age I loved to dance, and whenever he began to play the piano I was on my feet, twirling around. I knew that all I wanted to be was a ballet dancer.

Manners and etiquette were important to my parents and they were quite strict with all of us about behaviour, especially at meal times, but we were a very loving family and they had the utmost trust in us. It wasn't always totally justified, I'm afraid. We lived next door to a spinster who was a bit of an ogre and some children in the square used to tease her, banging on her door and running away. I didn't do that but I was fascinated by some particular plants she had in her garden. The leaves were silver, furry and so soft. I used to sneak through a hole in the fence and pick them. I just wanted to touch them. One day she got very angry and marched round to my mother complaining she'd seen me in her garden again. My mother immediately sprang to my defence saying, 'My daughter wouldn't do something like that,' and turned to me for confirmation. With an angelic face I insisted, 'No Mummy, I didn't.' She trusted me.

We didn't have relatives nearby and my parents didn't tend to entertain at home. Outside of our immediate family the most important person was my grandmother on my father's side. Her husband, my grandfather, had died before I was born, but Granny was fit as a fiddle. At regular intervals we would all pile into the car, another Vauxhall (my father stayed loyal to the same make of car all his life) and trek up to Grimsby to see her. Granny lived in a small bungalow and when we stayed it was a bit of a tight fit, so she shared her room and her bed with me.

One year we spent Christmas with her. I hung my pillowcase at the end of my bed, ready for Father Christmas to come and fill it up. At that age I believed totally and completely in the whole business and I was so excited it was difficult to get to sleep. I was just beginning to doze off when I heard the door open and a heavy tread of footsteps. It sounded as if someone had come right into the room. 'It's Him,' I thought, freezing in anticipation and scrunching my eyes tight shut. 'He's come too early and doesn't realise I'm not asleep yet.'

There was a pause, during which I hardly dared breathe and the sound of something being moved. Then I heard the same heavy tread as the footsteps went out again. I don't know how long I lay there with my eyes closed before I finally fell asleep but I was much too terrified to look, which was just as well. I would have been desperately disappointed to find the pillowcase still empty. Years later, when the disappointing truth about Father Christmas was finally revealed to me, I realised those heavy treads had simply been my grandmother coming into the room as she began her preparations for bedtime. It was my mother, waiting until she was absolutely sure I was asleep, who would have crept in much later to fill the pillowcase. As it was, the magic act was accomplished and when I woke early next morning, the case was satisfyingly lumpy with lots of parcels.

My grandmother's bungalow was an old-fashioned place, to my young eyes, with plants in the porch and a parlour kept beautifully for visitors and never used otherwise. She had a piano in that room which my father would sometimes play when we visited. While we were in Grimsby we would also go out and about visiting my mother's relatives. She had two sisters and a brother living in the area – Aunty Betty, Aunty Nell, Uncle Owen and Uncle John. My mother was particularly close to Aunty Nell.

The whole question of our adoption was handled very cleverly by my mother. We simply grew up with that knowledge as part of our consciousness, so I could never pinpoint when we didn't know and when we did know. She must have talked about it quite naturally from our earliest days. I can remember she was confident enough to make jokes as well, saying, 'Oh why did we get *you* from the nursing home!' in a teasing, loving way if I was being particularly difficult.

Nevertheless the subject did begin to preoccupy me as I got older and became more aware that other children were not adopted like me. I used to think: 'Why me? I'm different and I'm odd.' That had a great bearing on me as a child as I compared myself to other children. You'd think it would make me feel closer to Alistair and Roddy, as we shared the same experience, but it didn't.

I began to fantasise about my real parents. My favourite dream was that my mother was a ballet dancer. I often wondered where she was, who she was and what she looked like. On some occasions I would ask my mother: 'Well, what was she like?' but it wasn't something I could say easily to her – it was clear she didn't want to talk about it and therefore it was embarrassing. She would always give me the same response: 'We don't know anything dear, we just don't know anything. We've got you now and we love you.' So it was something that I could never really get clear answers about, a taboo subject. In fact it became an area of my life that I couldn't talk about to anyone at all. As a child I never told other children I was adopted. It was a secret, something I couldn't admit because I thought they would be shocked and wouldn't like me any more. It made me feel quite lonely because even fantasies about my mother had to be secret. I had a rich inner world that was very private. I was an imaginative child, idealistic with lots of romantic thoughts. At that stage I never contemplated actually meeting my real mother because it never occurred to me that it would be possible. I was adopted, Kathleen and Donald were my parents and that was what I accepted.

In the same way I never questioned the Catholic religion. Dressing up, going to Mass each Sunday and having a roast Sunday lunch afterwards was a tradition my parents never varied. So too were the prayers and services at the convent I started to attend while we were in Cardiff. My greatest fear, once I started school, centred around the little bottles of milk with straws that we were given to drink at break-time. The rule was that we had to finish the whole bottle and on more than one occasion I couldn't manage this. When this happened I was made to stand out in the playground while I drained the bottle to the last drop. Soon my anxiety about the whole ritual reached such a pitch that I only had to see the little bottles stacked in their crates outside the classrooms at the start of each day to begin to feel sick.

When I was seven we left Cardiff and moved to Northern France, to a beautiful house in a village called Samois sur Seine, near Fontainebleau. We had a very pretty large French house with shutters and a veranda, set on the banks of the River Seine. The house had wooden balconies and a porch with a narrow road running in front of it, though there was barely any traffic. Beyond were the grassy banks of the river. The sitting room was upstairs, to optimise the view, and there was a beautiful garden with a huge weeping willow tree and a big orchard.

I loved it there; I think the whole family did. Alistair and I learned to row and handle boats as my father had two moored on the river: one rowing boat and another with a small motor. You could watch the barges going past on the river. In those days there were lots of people who lived and worked on the barges and even kept chickens on them for fresh eggs. When the chickens stopped laying frequently, they'd be chucked on to the bank. This often happened outside our house, where the river was narrow, and

I would run down and pick them up to take home and keep as pets in the garden. We had quite a collection after a while.

Our stay in France was the only time I didn't go to a convent as there wasn't one nearby. Instead Alistair and I went to the International School where there were children from all different backgrounds, but especially from the services. My teacher was a very quiet English lady and for some reason I was her pet and used to sit next to her. I was mostly quiet and shy too, so perhaps that's why we liked each other, but I did have a fiery streak even in those days. Alastair was a sweet-natured boy who didn't like confrontation or upset. One day some boys began throwing stones at him in the playground and I ran up screaming and shouting, and stood in front of him saying, 'Don't you throw stones at my brother!' Although I was smaller than them, my fury made them back off.

As Roddy turned from a baby to a toddler and then a little boy, the dynamics of our family changed slightly, with Roddy being co-opted into roles in Alistair's 'boy' games more and more. Maid Marion seldom had star billing any longer and was finally dropped from the cast list. I didn't mind particularly because by now I had begun to make friends with girls my own age from other Army families posted there. I had a particular friend called Susan Strong who lived down the road and whose father was also in the Army. I was doll mad and we used to play with our dolls at either her house or mine. One day we were playing in her bedroom when

I got a Spangle sweet stuck in my throat and started choking. I was so shy of other people's parents that the idea of telling her parents, who were just downstairs, that I was in trouble was out of the question. I simply fled from her house and ran the few yards down the road to mine bursting into the sitting room where my parents were. By now I was red in the face and spluttering. My father immediately realised what was happening and turned me upside down, shaking me until I managed to cough up the sweet. Another friend from those days was called Helen Vallie, whose father was also in the Army, and she was to play an unexpected role later in my life.

After two years, which was the normal period for a posting, we moved back to England, and settled in another rented house, this time in Bushey, Hertfordshire. It was a nice four-bedroom detached house in a quiet cul-de-sac, with fields at the bottom of a good-sized garden. The move meant another new school but I didn't mind; continually moving around was what I was used to. I made friends easily and wasn't worried about being the new girl again. By now my younger brother and I were old enough to get the bus from outside our house to travel the short distance to Rosary Priory Preparatory School in Bushey Heath, which was a private Catholic school. It was very firmly impressed on me that Roddy was my responsibility and my mother was always worried in case I forgot to collect him when it was time to get the bus home. Alistair went off to boarding school at Belmont Abbey in

Herefordshire, a Benedictine school, which he didn't particularly enjoy. The first time he came home he made a big fuss about having to go back again and would much rather have stayed at home with me and Roddy.

Our school was in a large Victorian house which is today home to Immanuel College, a mixed secondary school. Whereas the international school in France had no uniform, my mother loved my uniform at Rosary Priory. In winter I wore a royal blue blazer, a pinafore dress and a dark blue velour hat to go with a dark blue coat. In summer I wore a cotton dress and a straw panama hat with a blazer. I took my first Holy Communion at the local Catholic church at the age of eight, dressing up in the traditional white dress and carrying a prayer book.

Imaginary games were what I loved most, although I'm afraid I had a tendency to want them to be my games and often as not played at my house. Our big garage, empty when my father took the car to work, was an ideal place to turn into a palace, a dungeon or other make-believe setting. Grown-ups were not allowed in, lest they break the spell or, more likely, told me to take my friends up to my bedroom. As a precaution against such interference I would always lock the door from the inside. 'What are you doing, Fiona?' my mother would ask through the keyhole when she came to check on us and found her way barred. Outside, backing on to the garage, was a row of three coal and wood bunkers and on one occasion I persuaded three of my friends to let me shut them inside. 'You've just got to go in here for five minutes, it's only five minutes,' I explained. Amazingly they all thought it was great fun and squeezed inside the bunkers through the little doors, letting me lock them in. Fortunately my mother didn't arrive before I had time to release them.

When friends weren't around my little brother Roddy was a willing participant in my games. We had a stone-flagged floor in the kitchen and when I went through a phase of thinking I'd like to be a teacher, it made an ideal substitute for a blackboard. 'Now,' I'd address Roddy, chalking my sums all over the tiles, 'two and two are? What's the answer?'

When the usual two-year posting was up we moved again. I was ten and approaching my last year of primary school. Our next location was Woking in Surrey where we lived in the army barracks. This time our home was very grand. My father had been promoted to the rank of colonel. Driving through an archway into a broad cul-de-sac of houses, the brigadier's house was the most magnificent, set right at the end, but ours was big too and set next door. Vittoria House was a huge Victorian house with spacious, high-ceilinged rooms and a beautiful garden backing on to woods. We each had our own bedroom and there was lots of excitement and a good feeling around at that time. A strict hierarchy was observed in the layout of the housing. All the soldiers and warrant officers' quarters were set at the other end and we were expected to observe this segregation in our friendships too. Although I often played with a girl whose father was a warrant officer, I was never allowed to bring her back to the house. My father always wanted to know what someone's background was and what their father did. Odd really when you think he had taken on three children whose own backgrounds he can only have had the vaguest idea about.

Both my parents loved us all dearly, but as I grew older I think I was to become something of a source of mystery and surprise to them, especially to my mother.

chapter three

Boys, Boys, Boys

It was my first day at boarding school and I was in the playground trying to persuade one of the girls to do something as part of a game I wanted to play. One of the nuns on duty came over and asked: 'What's your name, dear?'

'My name's Fiona,' I said, looking up at her.

'And you're a very bossy little girl, aren't you?' she observed.

I was shocked, not least because it was true. I'm afraid I was a bossy little girl. It was a trait that had emerged when I was growing up in France. My girlfriends there used to call me Bessy Bossy Boots because I was always trying to organise them into the imaginary games I wanted to play. Yet alongside the extrovert, bossy side I presented was a secretive, insecure side. I had grown up being used to keeping secrets and it had already become second nature to hide my real feelings.

Boarding school made the biggest impact on my life. I went away when I was ten years old to St Antony's, the prep school for a Catholic Convent called Leweston School in the Dorset town of Sherborne. My father drove my mother and I there with my huge trunk in the boot. The school was housed in a beautiful eighteenth-century Palladian manor house with a very ancient chapel that pre-dated the manor house by about two hundred years, and some modern extension blocks. I stood in-between my parents as my father lifted the iron knocker on the imposing double wooden doors. The noise echoed away into the building, the doors opened and nuns came scurrying out along the gleaming marble floors to welcome us. This was the visitors' entrance where pupils were never allowed.

We were ushered into the Mother Superior's private rooms and tea and little cakes were brought for us. Then we were taken on a tour. In the hall was a magnificent sweeping marble staircase. Later I was to learn this was sacred territory and if any girl were caught daring so much as to step on the first stair they were in big trouble. There was a music room and a library as well as all the usual school rooms. The grounds were immaculately maintained with sweeping lawns and ancient spreading trees.

My parents came up with me to the little dormitory. I sat on the bed while my mother unpacked everything, opening and shutting drawers, saying, 'I've put your knickers in there and your vests in here.' I felt a bit numb and as it came closer and closer to saying goodbye I began to cry. I had always known it was going to happen and I was excited in some way, but the emotion at the moment of parting overcame me. My mother had put my name down when I was a little girl, and I had seen Alistair go off to boarding school at the age of eight. Private education for your children was one of the biggest perks of being an officer. My parents weren't rich, in fact managing money was the one area of his life where my father was rather hopeless, but they chose the best possible schools for us because it was all subsidised by the Army. It was without doubt a privileged education.

My great love still was dancing and when we moved from Bushey I had pleaded with my parents to send me to Elmhurst Ballet School, where girls could combine ballet with academic work from the age of 11 through to 16. I had a talent but my mother was completely against the idea of a career as a professional dancer. It simply wasn't something she could imagine. 'Oh you won't like that,' she insisted whenever the subject was raised. 'It's not suitable, it's an awful life.' Her doubts about the security of life as a dancer were shared by my father; both considered it too risky. I pleaded and pleaded with them but this was one battle I couldn't win. They wanted me to have a conventional education, at least to O-level standard (this was in the days before GCSEs came in). So, along with all the girls at Leweston, I had one session of ballet a week and, as something of a compromise, it was arranged that I would have extra private tuition.

My love of dancing was, I suppose, the distinguishing factor about me as far as my fellow pupils and the teachers were concerned during my adolescent years. Consequently I became known as 'the ballet dancer'. At the end of each year we put on a production and from the beginning I was given important roles. The first major part I had was in the *Nutcracker Suite*, in which I played three different roles – though not the lead because I was only 13. It was when I was 16 that I had my first starring role as 'The Snow Queen'.

It was another story altogether with my progress in music, however. I had loved playing duets with my father, who had encouraged and taught me at home to begin with, but unfortunately it all ground to a halt in my first year at the senior school. I was frightened of my piano teacher. She had an austere manner and wore a rather obvious grey wig, the combined effect of which was to make her seem slightly strange to me. In addition, the pianos for us to practise on, as opposed to the pianos in the music room where we had lessons, were in the changing rooms. This meant my stumbling attempts to master a new piece turned into very public performances as classes of older girls streamed in and out, chatting and laughing as they got ready for games. I was very self-conscious and felt they must be laughing at me. So because I hardly practised, I came to dread the lessons.

'Naughty, naughty girl!' my teacher would exclaim, tapping my hands every time I played a wrong note, which was frequently. Every time I wrote home or saw my parents I would beg my father:

'Please, let me give up piano.' Of course he couldn't fully understand why something I had loved and shown such enthusiasm for had turned into something I dreaded. 'Don't give up,' he'd say. 'You've got a nice touch.' So I had to persevere, but things didn't get any better and finally, after I reached grade four at the end of the second year, he gave in and agreed that I could drop the feared piano lessons.

Our lives in the convent were quite protected. The message, both explicitly in the form of warnings and also unspoken in the nuns' expectations of our behaviour, were that boys were nasty creatures who we shouldn't think about or have any contact with. Neither my father nor my mother ever spoke to me about sex, although when I was ten my mother raised the subject of periods in a manner intended to be casual and relaxed but which was typically embarrassed and tense.

'You might get a bit of blood,' she said one day as she sorted the laundry, the knickers she was folding implying where evidence of this mysterious event might manifest itself.

'If you do, come and tell me because I've got these things, STs, sanitary towels.' She then proceeded to show me, in one of her drawers, a pile of what looked like little white mattresses for tiny dolls.

Nor were there any explicit talks about sex at school, so it was left to the Girls Who Knew, and even at the prep school there were plenty of those, to initiate the rest of us. More preoccupying however, in my first years at senior school, than what you did or didn't do with boys, was the vital question of who could or couldn't use a tampon. In the privacy of the school bathroom I stood over a mirror with a pot of Vaseline and the little sheet of diagrams contained in each box. How? Where? As the rest of the dormitory began to bang impatiently on the door, I gave up. It was a magic trick I couldn't master for the time being.

I was a curious child. No, it was more than that. I was insatiably nosy. If there was a secret lurking I simply had to discover what it was. Every Christmas my parents would hide our presents, all wrapped up and labelled, in the top of a cupboard in their room. Before Christmas Day I would sneak in, nose around until I found the ones with my name on and very carefully unwrap them until I could discover what was inside. Then I'd seal them back up and put them away again. Consequently I always knew what I was getting and Christmas never held any surprises for me; that's how awful I was. It seems so silly and embarrassing that I spoiled the surprise, but I *had* to! I was so curious.

It was the same curiosity that led me to discover something more secret than Christmas presents. During my first summer holiday home from the convent one day I found myself alone in the house. Alistair was at a friend's house and Roddy had gone out shopping with my mother. My father was at work. I mooched around the house and, not even sure what I was looking for, went into my parents' bedroom. All children have a desire around this stage to discover their parents' secrets and in my life there was one big secret that I felt sure their room would contain clues to. The dominant piece of furniture was a huge, old, dark wooden wardrobe and it was to this that I was drawn. On the floor of the wardrobe, pushed towards the back, was a square tin box, painted black. It was fastened with a catch and a padlock. Suddenly I heard the sound of the front door opening and jumped back, shut the wardrobe door, and was out of the room in a flash.

What could be inside that needed locking up and hiding away? I was scared of getting caught but, at the same time, irresistibly drawn to the box. I visited the room and the wardrobe to peek at that box several more times. What would happen if I touched it? Then, one day, I pulled the box out. To my amazement and terror the hook and the body of the padlock slid easily apart. It was not locked after all. I was conscious of my heartbeat and my limbs felt wobbly. I lifted the iron lid. I'm not sure what I was expecting but, inside, at first glance, was just a boring collection of papers, old chequebook stubs and envelopes. My parents' dark blue hard-backed passports were slipped down one side. I shut the lid quickly and put the box, which was quite heavy, back into the wardrobe, careful to place it in exactly the same position.

I didn't see the picture of the grave for a long time. I was drawn to the box and used opportunities when I had the house to myself to go and look inside it, but I was also frightened of getting caught. As I got bolder I began to take things out of envelopes and read the contents. The picture of the grave was inside an envelope with a foreign stamp, together with a letter. It was a little black-and-white snapshot showing a headstone where the name Catherine Inglis could be clearly read, and the location, Cyprus. There was also a date: 1959. I knew immediately this was the grave of a little girl who had been stillborn to my mother. When I was very small I had once asked my mother why she hadn't had her own babies. She told me the only baby she'd had, a girl, had been born dead. I accepted this at the time in the way small children do, with a brief feeling of sadness but no real understanding. Later, I wanted to ask more questions, but I understood intuitively from my mother's manner at the time that questions would not be welcome. From the letter that accompanied it, which talked about the upkeep of the grave, I knew the picture was a desperately sad memento of that little girl. Eventually I realised that it was my parents' grief at this tragedy that had prompted them to search out a third child to adopt while we were in Cyprus, adding Roddy to their family.

I never spoke to my two brothers about my secret delving or about the things I found, even though I saw letters and knew things about both of them they did not know themselves. I instinctively knew they wouldn't approve, and might even tell my parents. Besides, it wasn't to discover secrets about them that I was hunting. I wanted to know about *my* birth, about clues to my beginning. I thought I would find my birth certificate but it wasn't there. My delving was not prompted by any unhappiness with my parents. Quite the reverse: I was very happy and didn't imagine the woman who had given me away as a baby even existed in the same world as mine. I was simply digging around in the inquisitive way young teenagers do, wanting to discover secrets about adult life.

Then, when I was about 13 and able to understand more about the contents of the box, I did find something. It was a long, cream-coloured book of tokens for free milk, presumably courtesy of the Department of Health, and in the front was a name: Audrey McCormack. I knew immediately it was my mother's name. I had known her name was Audrey because my mother had mentioned it once and it had stuck in my head. Below was an address. It was very simple: just a house number, a street name, and Leeds (this was in the days before postcodes). I didn't write any of it down. I didn't need to. I had no thoughts at that time that I would ever search out or find her. It never even occurred to me that she was living her life somewhere in England. She might as well have been living on another planet. Still, I was pleased to find something that was about me and the area of my life that was unknown.

I had never met anyone else who was adopted, or who owned up to or knew they were adopted, but as I grew older I told some of my friends at school about my background. My friends were important to me, and became especially so once I reached 15 and found the restrictions of life at the convent frustrating. It was a very narrow life with no freedom and nothing that could be of particular interest to teenagers. Above all, it was an all-female environment and around this time of course I had become interested in boys. In fact, I should say that interested is too mild a word. We convent girls were positively obsessed with boys. Any stray workmen of vaguely eligible age (that meant not white-haired and walking with a stick!) unlucky enough to stray into the convent grounds would come in for the closest attention.

Consequently when some building work had to take place to construct a new church big enough to seat 400 people, it was a major event. The workmen were treated to us hitching our skirts up, giggling and generally flirting as much as we could while the nuns tried to hustle us along to our classrooms. When the nuns weren't around the younger workmen used to respond with a few wolf-whistles, which made our day. One day my headmistress caught me waving at one of the lads and she gave me an on-the-spot lecture. 'You don't come to this school if you like mucking about with boys,' she said and was so furious that I truly believed what I'd been doing was terribly wrong and sinful.

When I was 15 my father was posted to Blandford Camp so, as they were now living only 25 miles from the school, I became a weekly border. I was delighted because the weekends were the most tedious time in the convent. My parents had come down to take me out as often as possible because apart from going to church and, as a treat, being allowed to watch a bit of television on Saturday evening, there was nothing to do. It was a very short weekend but going back home even briefly was wonderful. Every Saturday my father would arrive at 12 o'clock, after we had finished morning lessons, in his Vauxhall (my mother never learnt to drive), and take me back to the house in Blandford. On Sunday we had to be back at the school at seven o'clock and from lunchtime onwards on Sunday I had a horrible feeling of dread about the approaching curfew.

I didn't have many friends locally, on account of boarding, so my parents always let me bring a friend back with me at the weekend. Naturally they all wanted to come and I suddenly became everyone's best friend. The whole week at school was spent planning what we would do come Saturday. In fact we did very little, but compared to weekends at school my brief trips home were thrilling. We would stay in, gossip, watch TV, and walk up to Bryanston during the day. Bryanston was a large boys' public school in the days before it went co-ed, on the outskirts of Blandford. From the town centre, where our house was, there was a footpath that ran out of the town, through the woods by the River Stour and, eventually, after a two or three mile walk, alongside the borders of the school grounds. The pupils were allowed to use this path to walk into town and it was here that we'd get chatting to them. It was the highlight of our week.

I had what I *called* boyfriends when talking to my girlfriends at school, but it was all very innocent. Teenage fashion was so different to the way it is now and I was still very much a little girl, even at 15. Sometimes one of the boys would write to me. Letters were a supremely important part of boarding-school life. Every morning at breakfast the headmistress or the mistress on duty would stand with the post and call out everyone's names as she handed out the envelopes. If you didn't get any post it was awful. My mother wrote to me regularly, but I would sit there with sweaty hands, feeling really nervous and wondering if I was going to get a letter. When I heard my name I was so excited in case it was from a boy at Bryanston. If your name got read out two or three times it was very impressive and a sign of popularity. The names were read out over the microphone: Clare Ingalls, Jane Happen... what a ritual. I kept all my mother's letters.

The first boy I could really call my boyfriend was at Bryanston and his name was Bo. I met him on one of our trips along by the river and we began exchanging letters. I invited him back to our house to have tea and meet my parents. He was terribly polite and my parents liked him. Friendships between teenagers at boarding schools were common because none of us had many local friends, being away all the time. My father, who had always been protective of me, became even more watchful as I moved into the teenage years. Sometimes he embarrassed me, wanting to know who my friends were and where they came from, but deep down I felt safe knowing he cared so much. As a small child I had been a real Daddy's Girl, insisting on sitting next to him when we went out anywhere, and I was still very close to him.

On one of the few occasions when I met up with a local boy from the town my father's antennae were on full alert. There was a garage down the end of our road and this particular lad used to clean cars on a Saturday. He was at college and a year or so older than me. As I walked past the garage he always said hello. I was very shy but I liked him and after a while I stopped to chat. One day he plucked up the courage to ask me to go to the cinema with him that evening. I said yes and was terribly excited. When I came home I pleaded with my parents to let me go and my father said, 'He's got to come to the house to pick you up. I want to meet him first.' The poor boy, who was as shy as I had been, didn't know what hit him. My father, who always smoked a pipe, sat there puffing away and giving him the third degree: 'What film? What time does it start? What time will you be back...?' Not surprisingly it rather put him off. We scarcely spoke but just sat awkwardly in the cinema, watched the film and then he hurried me back to my house. It was not the most romantic of dates.

My parents never put any pressure on either me or my brothers about exams or what we aimed to do. They just wanted us to be happy, but I had my own driving ambitions. It had always been my aim to become a ballet dancer and when I was 16 I applied to the Royal Ballet School, with my parents' backing this time. We had to get some professional photographs done in different poses as part of the first stage of the application. I got through that and my father took me up to London for the audition. My teacher had given me every encouragement and led me to believe I stood a chance, but when I got there I realised I was so limited in what I could do. Against the girls from dedicated ballet schools I was totally lost. I changed into my pale pink tights, costume and hair net with half a dozen other girls and then we were called into a vast practise room with mirrors along one wall and a row of adjudicators sitting on chairs. We knew in advance what movements we had to perform and we all had to do them together. Immediately I realised I was out of my depth. The ability and standard of the girls from ballet schools was way ahead of mine with my once-a-week lesson. I wasn't in the same league. I tried my best to keep up but some of the things we were asked to do were quite beyond anything I had been taught.

I was terribly disappointed and felt a bit let down. My ballet teacher had really hyped me up, encouraging me and making me believe I had a chance. It also brought back memories of all those battles with my parents when I was 11 and wanted to go to ballet school, as these girls had. They told us straight away which girls should come back for another stage of audition so I knew immediately and wasn't surprised. I felt very despondent and it shattered my confidence completely. I lost heart in my ability to make it as a dancer and because I'd set my heart so totally on the Royal Ballet, I couldn't see another goal. My teacher urged me not to give up, and to try for a place with the Ballet Rambert or the Arts Education Trust, but I just felt that if I couldn't get to the Royal

Ballet School I didn't want what I saw as second best. It was silly of me to think like that, I know, but from that point on I just gave up on ballet as a career.

I was never one of the really rebellious ones at school but I flirted on the fringes of trouble. A group of us got in with these so-called hippies in Sherborne. Really they were just local lads living in a commune but they seemed much more exciting than the boys from Bryanston. Some of my friends had met them in the town and used to sneak out of school, going across the fields, to see them. I never actually went to the commune, though some of my friends did. But one day someone split on them. The headmistress went down to the house in a sort of solo raid which, with hindsight, was quite a courageous thing to do, and knocked on the door. One of her pupils, a friend of mine, answered the door. The headmistress went ballistic and the girls inside the house were expelled instantly. One of these was a very close friend of mine called Jo Hart, who I often got up to all sorts of mischief with, earning us the nickname The Terrible Twins. The headmistress wanted to know if there was anyone else who had associated with these boys and my name came up, along with a friend of mine called Bindy, which was short for Belinda. We weren't expelled but we were 'rusticated', which meant being sent home in disgrace for half a term. We had to endure a lecture in her study first. We were 'naughty, naughty girls associating with those filthy men in that filthy hovel'. My father came to collect me and I went home with a dark cloud over my head.

My mother was very conservative by nature and her overriding instinct was to protect me and keep me safe. That I seemed to rush headlong into all sorts of scrapes was a source of constant anxiety to her. She also found it hard to express her emotions and when she was embarrassed she concealed this by putting on a front or getting slightly prickly. Her attitude when I arrived home in disgrace was, 'Here we go again. *Boys*.' She loved me devotedly yet there was no doubt that I was also something of a mystery to her. The letters she wrote to me at school often began, 'Fiona, you really are the limit', usually in response to a plea for more money as I had blown a whole term's pocket money in three weeks or something of that nature. As I got older I realised our very different personalities were also a source of fascination to her and perhaps she admired some aspects of my character that she found hard to express in herself. However, her feelings were always tinged with anxiety about what I would do next. Not unjustifiably, as things frequently did go wrong and then she and my father would have to bail me out, which they always did. She certainly found my brothers a lot easier and more straightforward to manage.

After that episode I went back to school for a final year to do exams. At first all the other girls refused to speak to either Bindy or me as we were thought to be such a disgrace and we were 'sent to Coventry'. Fortunately they didn't keep it up longer than a week or so but it was a bit miserable. I left school with four O-levels but after ballet had been written off I didn't know what I wanted to do.

It was the summer of 1973: hemlines were climbing ever higher and like half the other teenagers in Britain I wanted to celebrate a new freedom where youth ruled. All around me the conventions and restrictions of the 1950s and post-war Britain which had ruled my parents' lives were being dumped unceremoniously in the dustbin of history. But how should I take the first steps to freedom?

chapter four

My Life, My Way

On my first morning at Poole Technical College, the lecturer walked into the classroom and I automatically went to stand up. Just in time I checked my reaction. All around me the other members of the class were not only remaining seated, they were totally ignoring the member of staff and carrying on chatting. After years at the convent, where we not only stood up when our teachers entered the room but automatically greeted them with the utmost politeness, I was totally embarrassed. It seemed such terribly bad manners to ignore the person who'd come to teach us.

That wasn't the only shock. I'd been living in a slightly unreal world, with the Army paying for a privileged education and my parents being so protective. Life at Poole Tech was a bit of an eye-opener. The building was dilapidated and hideous, a typical sixties block with a flat roof. My fellow students were also a real mixed crowd. I had been ready to ditch any kind of further education completely and take my chances finding a job, but my mother, ever cautious, was adamant I had some kind of training and steered me towards the safety of a secretarial course. I suggested a trendy college in Oxford, my parents suggested Poole Tech. The Army subsidy didn't extend to further education and there was no money for private fees, so my parents won.

On my first day one boy in particular stood out. His name was Norman and he wore a black cape, black leathers and drove a black motorbike. I immediately found his refusal to conform attractive and he began giving me lifts on the back of his bike. I discovered that, like me, he'd been to private school, which put us in a distinct minority at the college. However, what I didn't deduce for quite a time was that he was somewhat emotionally unstable. He began to get possessive and this turned into a form of obsession with me. If I walked slightly behind him instead of directly by his side, he'd get cross. He began to behave more and more as if he owned me. This was my first real adult relationship and although I was very confused about his behaviour, I didn't see at first how odd it was. But then he started to phone our home at all hours and my father had to ask him to stop calling all the time. When I tried to disentangle myself from him, he threatened to kill himself on his motorbike. I was frightened.

One day, towards the end of the first year, we had an argument outside the college. He slapped me across my face and I became completely hysterical, in the way teenage girls can. There was such a scene that the head came out and took me inside to calm down in the sick bay. While I was there little notes began to appear under the door from Norman saying how much he loved me and how sorry he was. I was so mad I tore them up. He began to wait outside my lectures and shadow me continually. I didn't tell my parents everything because I didn't want to worry them, but they guessed there was a problem. In the end I asked my parents if I could leave after a year and, having been aware there was something wrong, they agreed.

Although I hadn't completed the course I could type well and had learned Pitman shorthand. Now, finally, I wanted to finish with classrooms and teachers and get out into the world to live my own life. While it seems hard to believe now, the idea of careers for girls, outside secretarial and nursing, was pretty new. My own mother had stopped working when she married my father, in common with most women of her generation. As far as I was concerned she felt she had done her duty by seeing me through at least a year of the secretarial course and neither she nor my father put any pressure on me to commit to a career.

All of which was just as well. I was headstrong, determined to do things my way, and my primary aim was simply to have a whale of a time. Together with my great mate and former partner in crime from school days, Jo Hart, I hatched a plan to move to Bournemouth. It wasn't exactly Swinging London, but the nearest the South-West had to offer in the way of bright lights and sophisticated living, and a whole lot better than sleepy Blandford.

The Bournemouth evening paper was a source for both jobs and flats and we pored over it, circling likely looking ads. Fortunately in this boom era, jobs were plentiful and my confidence was boosted when I went for an interview with a firm of Bournemouth estate agents seeking a secretary and landed the job. Jo too was successful in getting work. The idea of unemployment and not being able to get work was quite unthinkable to my generation, who had never experienced the depression of the thirties.

We answered an ad placed by two young men training as architects, who were finding it hard to make ends meet and had decided to share a bedroom, freeing up a spare room to sub-let. Unfortunately the young men harboured a secret fantasy – not of wild living and free love but of the kind of domestic orderliness and hot meals they had known at home. Taking in two girl tenants would, they felt, miraculously resolve the tiresome business of cleaning, shopping and cooking. Sadly for them, neither Jo nor I were remotely domesticated. While the boys' room was mildly messy, ours quickly resembled a jumble sale. Clothes spilled out of the tiny wardrobe, washing accumulated on the floor and the bathroom was soon littered with sachets of Hint of a Tint shampoo, Mary Quant Peepers eyeshadow and Bare foundation.

When the boys began to complain that we never put the dustbins out or washed up, we went back to the small ads and quickly found a flat to rent with a bedroom each. Mine was decorated in deep red: walls, curtains and carpet. I thought it wonderfully Bohemian after the subdued pastels of my parents' home. Our new flat meant that once we'd found the rent each month we hardly had any spare cash, but it was our first taste of freedom and we were happy. Outside work our time was spent window-shopping in Chelsea Girl, going to the pub or simply staying in, gossiping, giggling and watching *Ready Steady Go* on TV.

After about nine months, Jo quit her job working in a TV shop because it was too boring and went back home to think about starting some kind of training. I took a room in a shared house and after one disastrous week working in Chelsea Girl, I found another secretarial job. Soon, however, I realised that every secretarial job would grow to be predictable and routine. I took to scanning *The Times* and the *Telegraph* for something different. The answer came in an advertisement for a Harvest Maid to work on a farm in Marlborough, Wiltshire. It was such a funny-sounding job that it appealed. I drove over to Marlborough for an interview with the farmer, Mr Roberts. The farm was at the end of a long imposing drive, near the village of Manton. It wasn't really a farm in the way I had imagined. Certainly hay barns and sheds were nearby, but the impressive old house with sweeping lawns appeared more like a manor. The interview was something of a test in itself. Mr Roberts was a tall, imposing man in his forties which, to me, seemed ancient. As we shook hands I tried to look him in the eye and became aware that one of his eyes was fixed.

'You see I have a glass eye,' he said immediately, and as he began to ask me about myself it was clear he was testing whether I had the spirit and confidence to accept his somewhat eccentric manner.

'I sometimes like to take it out,' he challenged, cupping his hand in front of his eye and tilting his head forward as though he were going to roll it into the palm of his hand.

'That's all right,' I said and I honestly meant it. I didn't find him or his glass eye intimidating. My parents, and especially my mother, had instilled the confidence in me to be able to talk to anyone. When he saw I wouldn't be fazed, Mr Roberts relaxed somewhat and outlined the job.

Every summer he took in agricultural students to help with the harvest. My job would be to cook them breakfast in the morning and then make sandwiches at lunchtime and take them up to the fields. In addition he needed me to do some office work for him. He had a red Morgan sports car which he would insure for me so I could drive into town and do the shopping. It all sounded like fun. He explained that his wife had left him the year before and they had a young baby, a little girl who sometimes came back to stay with him and I might have to look after her now and again. I wasn't very baby-minded but I said that would be all right.

I moved in the next week and loved it immediately. My room in the farmhouse was tucked up under the eves and I would wake each morning to country sounds and a sense of happiness. At lunchtime I took sandwiches up to the students and farm workers in the fields and in the evening I prepared an evening meal. The huge farmhouse kitchen had an Aga and a long pine table where four students and I, with Mr Roberts at the head of the table, would sit to eat. Although I had never cooked for that number before I wasn't nervous. There were an awful lot of potatoes to peel but I made simple, wholesome dishes like casseroles and macaroni cheese.

It wasn't especially hard work and it was a lot of fun, too. My boss was a very sociable man and held croquet parties at weekends where we'd drink Pimms on the lawn. As time went by I learned that the wife who had left had actually been a previous Harvest Maid and wasn't his first wife. He liked woman and was rather flirtatious but he was always perfectly respectful with me and I continued to call him Mr Roberts. He took an interest in what I wanted to do in the future and because he knew I liked the area and didn't specially want to go home when the harvest season finished, he suggested that I become a farm secretary, working for a number of farms in the area. He also offered me rent-free accommodation in a little semi-detached thatched cottage he had in Marlborough, in return for doing some of his own office work and occasionally minding his baby daughter when she visited.

A pretty cottage of my own and a job with lots of variety sounded perfect. Just before I was about to move in, however, Mr Roberts decided he wanted to keep on one of his agricultural students who he considered especially talented. He asked if I would mind sharing the cottage, which had two bedrooms. From working at the farm I knew this boy, a marine biologist called Peter. He was pleasant and easy-going and the idea of ready-made company quite appealed. Peter was the best student Mr Roberts had ever had and he wanted to keep him on for another year.

I'm sure everyone in the village thought we were a married couple, especially when I had Mr Roberts's little girl for the day. The idea of a young man and woman sharing a place but not being romantically involved was novel. It was novel for us, too. We became great friends and then one night, after sharing a bottle of wine, we ended up in bed together. It sounds casual but it was a decision I took very seriously. Even though all around people were talking about free love, and the pill was easy to obtain, my years in a Catholic convent had been an influence. I was absolutely terrified of getting pregnant and spent my teenage years fighting off boys. I had gone in for some kissing and cuddling but at that stage I wasn't at all interested in a more serious physical relationship. Years later I discovered that the Bryanston boys used to make bets with each other about which one would be the first to sleep with me, which would have horrified me if I'd known at the time because in many ways I was very naive.

After Peter and I became lovers I took him home to meet my parents but I introduced him as a friend. As was my father's way, he immediately began to ask Peter what he planned to do with his life. Although Peter had a very good degree in marine biology he didn't have a career in mind and, true to form, my father immediately began extolling the virtues of a life in the Army.

'Why don't you join the Army? It's a very good career,' he'd begin in a speech that had become very familiar to me. My father was always trying to get people to join the Army and could be very persuasive about the benefits. After all, it had given him a good life.

We hadn't been living in the cottage long when a cold snap in the autumn weather made us decide to light a fire in the sitting room. There was no central heating and using the electric fire was very expensive. It was a day when I had Mr Roberts's little girl to look after and I was amusing her in the kitchen when I became aware of clouds of smoke drifting past the window. I called Peter and we stepped out into the backyard and looked up. Smoke was billowing, not from the chimney, but from a part of the thatched roof. It was clear the whole place was about to go up and by the time the fire brigade arrived, summoned by a neighbour with a phone, we were standing helplessly in the road, holding the toddler close, watching as the thatch blazed. The chimney breast, it was discovered, had a hole in the brickwork which allowed sparks to fly into the roof space and ignite the thatch.

By the time the fire brigade had finished with the cottage it wasn't fit to sleep in. We all decamped to the farmhouse but although it was only to be a temporary lodging place until the cottage was repaired, I decided that was a good point to leave.

Although I loved the area and was heavily involved with Peter, I had found a flaw in my role as a roving farm secretary. Mr Roberts had kindly put me in touch with several farmers and there was no shortage of work. It was simply that two of them had proved much more interested in my attractions as a 19-year-old girl than my efficiency with a typewriter. Flirtatious remarks I could deal with, but when one red-faced overweight fellow tried to kiss me it was another matter. We had ended up in what would have been a perfect comedy moment dodging around the table in his kitchen if I hadn't been genuinely scared. These farmhouses were very isolated. I escaped on that occasion by threatening to complain to Mr Roberts but in reality I couldn't mention it to him. These were his colleagues. It would have been embarrassing as well as impossible for him to resolve.

It was time to look for another job. Meanwhile, Peter made his own surprising decision. That meeting with my father obviously sowed some pretty potent seeds. Peter followed his advice and went on to join the Signals Regiment. We'd split up by this time, but our brief liaison played a rather key part in the direction of his life.

For me, it was back to scanning the *Times* small ads and I struck lucky with a job that took me away to Scotland for a year. It also led to my first experience of heartache and rejection. The family I joined wanted someone to live in, again on a farm, to help with office work in the morning and look after their two little boys, aged three and four, in the afternoon. Their mother was a keen rider and during the winter she loved to go out hunting several times a week. When that happened my job was to take the boys out somewhere. The location was very beautiful, in the south-west of Scotland in the Dumfries and Galloway region, not far from the sea and just outside a little town called Castle Douglas. I loved it from the beginning. They were a very nice couple, though I sometimes found their sons a bit of a handful, and they treated me as part of my family.

That was the first year when I was truly away from my parents, away from discipline for the first time in my life, and I let rip. The family suggested that in order to meet people I went along to the social events at the Young Farmers' club. The boys there were all landed gentry who had inherited or were about to inherit their parents' or their grandparents' farms. As well as the Young Farmers' club, I joined the local drama group and we put on a show in Troon. It was a variety show and we made up a funny dance routine which entailed one of the boys, who was very strong, lifting me up. Being the only English girl had a rarity value that seemed to add to my popularity and I had a ball. I dated so many boys and I was out practically every night. There were drinks in lovely country pubs, dinner in restaurants or sometimes at their homes, dances or balls where I learnt Scottish Dancing, and in the summer we went for picnics or water-skied.

It was on one of these water-skiing trips to a nearby lake that

I met Angus. I liked him immediately. He had a soft, educated voice with a gentle Scottish lilt, thick dark hair and a muscular build. He was also very charming, with a flirtatious, teasing style. We began going out and soon he invited me to visit his home. He drove me there and as we turned off the main road a series of increasingly small lanes led finally to an imposing entrance and a long drive. The evening was just turning to dusk and as we rounded the bend the most beautiful Scottish manor house came into view. Lights twinkled in the low, mullioned windows, ivy covered the grey stone walls, and inside a huge flagged stone hall led through to a pretty sitting room looking out across well-tended lawns.

It was a most enchanting place, set in a valley with hills rising gently on three sides. I assumed it was his parents' home, although that evening there was no sign of them. The chemistry between us was practically making sparks but Angus put no pressure on me to stay the night – an assurance which made him all the more attractive. I think we both knew we would become lovers. It was on my second visit there, when again there was no sign of anyone else, that I asked about his parents.

'Oh, they have their own home,' he said, naming an area some twenty miles away.

'This is my home, left to me by my grandmother who died last year.' I couldn't believe a boy of 25 could be living in such a splendid place all alone. He stood for everything I had fantasised about in terms of living in the country and owning animals and now it seemed the woman he married would be lady of the manor as well.

With the free rein of that enchanted manor, discreetly maintained, I was to discover, by a housekeeper, we embarked on a passionate affair. I fell deeply in love with Angus and he said that he loved me too. I've always loved the country and country life, which was also his life. The family bred beef cattle and I learned that they owned many thousands of acres of land. We even began to talk about a future together, and children.

After a few months he had to go away with his father to Argentina on a business trip. He was away for three weeks and I missed him terribly, counting the days until he got back. Strangely, on the weekend he should have been home, I heard nothing. I called several times before I got him on the phone. As soon as I heard him speak I knew something had changed. He told me he didn't think we should see each other, that it was better we went our own ways. I couldn't believe what I was hearing. I was distraught and totally crushed. I cried nearly every day and rang him several times in tears. Eventually I got a short note saying that he wasn't worth what I felt for him and I shouldn't waste my time on him.

To anyone versed in the ways of Scottish land-owning classes all this would have been immediately understandable. Indeed the family I was staying with tried to point out what had happened, saying things like, 'Angus is very influenced by his father' and 'When there's a lot of land at stake people are not always free to make up their own minds.' It wasn't until many years later that I was able to understand that Angus, with one large estate already and due to inherit an even larger chunk of Scotland, was not going to make a match with an English girl whose Army parents didn't even own their own home, never mind any land. At the time however, it was just a bitter rejection which completely broke my heart. I recovered sufficiently to pick myself up for the last couple of months there but when the year was up I wanted to come home, even though the family I was with invited me to stay longer. I felt, even without the disappointment of finishing with Angus, that I had enjoyed all the changing aspects of life in Scotland through a full year and that staying on would just mean repeating many of those experiences. My parents were very pleased I was coming back down south once more, and my father drove up in his trusty Vauxhall to collect me and the substantial amount of baggage I had amassed.

If my parents were pleased to have me home, it was also nice for me to be back with them again. My mother was dying to cosset me and fuss over me which was a treat after a year away. She immediately began to spoil me, doing all my washing and ironing, and bringing me cups of tea in bed. Looming over this cosy scene, however, was the question of what to do next. I still had no yearning for a career as such, preferring to look for work that would bring its own adventures. One day, not long after I got home, I heard about a really big adventure. A friend who had a boat moored in Poole Harbour told me the owner of a large ocean-going yacht was looking to get a crew together to sail his boat down to the Mediterranean. I was determined to apply.

'You'll hate it,' said my mother, who was worried sick about the risks involved.

'You haven't got enough experience,' said my father, more rationally, and it's true that my sailing experience had been confined to pottering about in small dinghies. But I was not to be deterred and succeeded, by virtue of my overwhelming enthusiasm and an almost equal amount of exaggeration about my sailing experience, in getting an interview. It turned out the trip was not scheduled for several months but against all the odds I was put on a shortlist of possible crew. My excitement was only matched by my mother's anxiety.

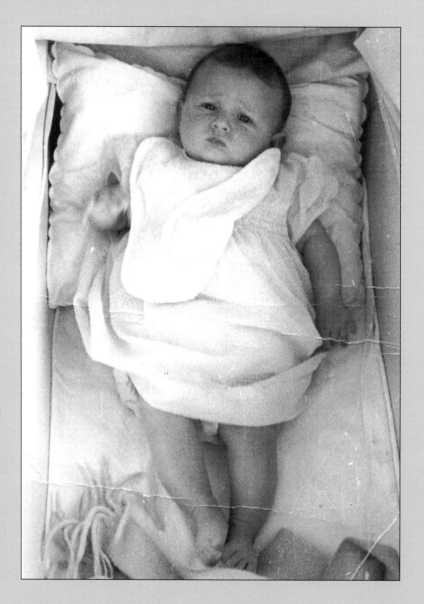

Me at six weeks. This is the photograph I took to show
Audrey at our first meeting, which was a duplicate
of the only photo she had of me.

Roddy, Alastair and me on a windswept outing
to the Brecon Beacons.

My first Holy Communion.

On the banks of the Seine with our rowing boat
when I was about eight or nine.

My mother Kathleen,
in her early twenties.

My handsome father,
Donald.

My parents' marriage in 1940, described by my
mother as 'Our hurried wedding'.

Duncan's Christening, May 1979, with the happy
grandparents.

Duncan filling up the paddling pool in the garden at High Trees.

chapter five

Summer of Love

The prospect of seeing her only daughter disappear on what to her seemed a hazardous mission, given my lack of sailing experience, sent my mother scurrying to study the jobs vacant columns in the papers. Since the trip was still some months off, she argued, I'd need a job in the meantime. Of course secretly she hoped to find something which would distract me from my mad crewing idea. So it came about, with my mother's prompting, that I answered an ad for a job that was my strangest one yet.

A couple in Somerset were looking for a young woman who would act as companion to their teenage daughter, which seemed a very Victorian idea but intriguing. When I enquired, it turned out they were worried that their daughter, who was an only child, was becoming very overweight and they thought a great deal of the problem was boredom. The idea that I would be paid simply for my entertainment value and to keep someone out of the fridge sounded too good to be true. I went to meet them and discovered that they lived in a very attractive house in a pretty but rather remote village. Their daughter, I'll call her Rebecca, was about two years younger than me and had a red MG sports car and a wardrobe full of the most beautiful designer clothes which, since she was two to three stone overweight, she couldn't get into. Fortunately I could. Although I'm not sure if this was really what her parents had in mind, we were soon zipping around the countryside in the MG and her social life had stepped up a gear or two.

Very soon into my strange but thoroughly enjoyable new job, an invitation arrived from Helen Vallie to her 21st birthday party. She was my childhood friend from France whose family had also moved to Dorset and were living in the pretty village of Corfe Castle. Our parents had stayed in touch and we'd been over to their house when they moved to Dorset. I didn't know anyone who would be at the party, apart from Helen, so as part of my job as social secretary and weight-watching buddy I invited Rebecca along. We got ready at my parents' house and I zipped myself into a skin-tight catsuit, raised my height a couple of inches with a pair of huge platform shoes and surveyed myself in the mirror. It was a new outfit and totally seventies: dark blue and made of very fine needlecord with huge bell-bottoms and a plunging zip front.

We drove over in the MG and arrived at the Vallies' house to find a big marquee set up on the lawn. It was a lovely summer evening and people were able to drift between the house and marquee or sit around in the gardens drinking and eating. The disco was held in the marquee and Rebecca and I took to the dance floor. Soon we were joined by two boys, so we were in pairs, but side by side. Halfway through the dance the boy my friend was dancing with asked his mate to swap and I got a new partner. His name was Simon Roscoe, he was nicely spoken and very charming. He wore jeans and a stripy shirt but what I particularly noticed were his clogs, because they were so different. He was cocky with a cheeky, impish face. I immediately found his flirtatious, confrontational manner exciting. We began trying to challenge and impress each other with little acts of daring and when he said he wanted some whisky, I said I knew where it was hidden. I led him off into the house in search of the drinks cabinet I knew was in the parquet-floored dining room.

As midnight approached Rebecca wanted to go as she had a long drive home. I had told my parents she would drop me back, but now I'd met Simon I didn't want to say goodbye. I reassured her I'd get a lift with someone else, although I hadn't the faintest idea who. Some time after midnight the party began winding down and Simon suggested that his friend and I came back for coffee at his flat in Swanage, a seaside town about half an hour away. His friend fortunately had a car. Another girl who wanted a lift to Swanage joined us and the presence of the other two took the tension out of the 'come back for coffee' invitation. Nevertheless, as Simon laid his arm along the back seat I felt blue sparks must surely be visible, so great was the electricity between us.

The house where he had an upstairs flat was owned by his grandmother, he explained, so we had to be quiet when we went in. In the darkness I could see it was a small Victorian house situated in a cul-de-sac. The girl who'd wanted a lift seemed to have abandoned the idea of heading for her own home so the four of us climbed the narrow stairs to Simon's flat, shushing frantically but also giggling and stumbling because we were a bit tipsy. Simon went off into a little kitchen, which was along a passage and down a couple of steps, and a minute later he was calling to me to come and help. How a man in his own house could seem helpless faced with the challenge of boiling a kettle and putting instant coffee into four mugs must have tested his acting skill, but he put on a convincing display of not knowing where anything was. Although we'd danced together earlier in the evening, suddenly being in that little kitchen, not touching but in such close physical proximity, was absurdly exciting. I made sure it was Simon who carried the tray back into the sitting room because I was sure that even if I didn't drop the whole tray, the sound of the coffee cups rattling would have been audible.

The album that had been huge the year before was *Rumours* by Fleetwood Mac and now Simon put that on. It was one that I especially loved and I took it as a good sign that we had similar taste. The flat was quite untidy and when Simon directed me to the bathroom I rather nosily took a peak into his bedroom on the way. At the end of the bed was a most unusual rocking-horse carved out of dark wood. On my return Simon said, 'At last, I thought you'd got lost.' I didn't tell him that getting in and out of my catsuit was an elaborate affair, instead I replied, 'I like your horse.' 'All the girls say that,' he joked and immediately I wished I hadn't foolishly fed him that line and that he hadn't fallen into making such a predictable innuendo. I began talking to the other two about the album. 'Dreams' was my favourite track and we talked about the singer, Stevie Nicks, who wrote that song after busting up with her boyfriend, Lindsey Buckingham.

Simon produced some bottles of wine and soon our conversation got more and more inane as we sat round in the semi-gloom staring at the gloopy bits of his lava lamp. I became aware that Simon's eyes, however, were focused on me rather than the lamp.

'Look at Fiona's catsuit, doesn't she look good in it,' drawled Simon. 'Come on, stand up and give us a twirl.' Emboldened by several glasses of wine I did as he asked. I was size 10, very slim, with long dark hair. I was showing off to Simon. He was challenging me to do so. It was our game of dares again and I happily took part.

We talked and drank and smoked our way through the small hours and finally all crashed out in his sitting room. When I awoke in a crumpled heap on the sofa it was light outside and the other two had left. Simon was standing in front of the fireplace, staring at me. He came over, crouched down in front of me and very slowly began to kiss me. I felt supercharged with the most powerful sexual attraction. Just touching him made me feel intensely alive.

'Stay here with me,' he said. I knew nothing beyond his name, we had spent just a few hours together and shared nothing more than a passionate kiss, but I knew it was the right thing to do.

'I need to go home and get my things,' I said. There was no phone in the flat so we went out in the Sunday morning quiet of Swanage to find a phone box. Simon waited outside while I rang home. My mother answered and I could hear relief in her voice, immediately followed by anxiety.

'Mum? It's me. The party was great. Look, I've met this boy. He's very special and he's asked me to stay with him.'

'What are you talking about? Don't be so stupid. Just come home, come home now.' She sounded angry. This was yet another act of madness from me, another of the impetuous twists and turns in my life that she found so hard to understand.

Yet I was now 21 years old, and as protective and caring as my parents were I knew had to live my own life, however wrong my decisions might sound to them. I instinctively felt I had to be with Simon and, at that point, everything else seemed irrelevant. I brushed aside my job, 'I'll phone them and they'll understand', and even the distant prospect of my sailing ambitions, which my mother must have been desperate even to mention. 'I probably wouldn't make it to the final crew, and anyway you didn't want me to do it,' I countered.

Simon offered to come with me to Blandford to collect some things. I agreed immediately as I knew his presence would make it more difficult for my mother to make a fuss. We took a taxi together and at midday I was back home, still dressed in my catsuit from the night before, smiling brightly and saying, 'I've just come to pack a bag.' Fortunately my father was not at home to give Simon the third degree and my mother simply didn't know what to say. Leaving Simon standing awkwardly in the kitchen with my mother I flew upstairs, hastily changed into jeans and a T-shirt, stuffed a few things in a bag and was down again in minutes.

'I'm off now,' I said and handed her Simon's address which I'd written out beforehand. Then we were out of the house and back into the taxi we'd kept waiting outside. On the drive back I felt nothing but excitement. Simon was very keen on me and yet I also had an awareness that he was used to attention being directed towards him. At that stage his arrogance appeared solely as a challenge.

By now this strange day was turning to evening and Simon leaned forward to give some directions to the taxi driver.

'Where are we going?'

'Somewhere I hope you'll like.' I did. We drove through country lanes and then up on to the downs beyond Swanage, arriving finally at a beautiful country pub.

Neither of us had eaten much and Simon was starving, although the adrenalin high I had been on all day made me pretty indifferent to food. When I said I didn't want anything to eat he fed me forkfuls off his plate and teased me about getting too thin. I told him about my series of mad jobs and he told me he was on the shortlist for a well-paid position in marketing that he hoped to get.

'Now, a walk,' he said finally, when we had shared another couple of glasses of wine. He obviously knew the area well. The light was beginning to fade by now and I felt just a thrill of danger as we climbed over a stile along from the pub, hid my bag in some bushes and set off across fields following a path towards the coast. It was the kind of beautiful midsummer evening that stretches on and on so that at half past nine the dusk was only just beginning to gather. There was no one else in sight as we scrambled down a path that opened out into a flat grassy area high above limestone cliffs with a stony beach below.

'This area is called Dancing Ledge, a long time ago it was a stone quarry. It's beautiful isn't it?' We stood hand in hand looking out across the darkening sea. It was an enchanted place, with downs rising slightly behind us and in front of us the wide sky and sea merging into one as darkness fell. Simon led me back from the edge and laid his jacket on the grass in a secluded dip hidden from view. The romance of the setting and the magnetism I felt between us made me a willing lover.

It was several days before he told me he loved me. I didn't care because withholding those words was part of a game we were playing. We were both challenging, vivacious people, and in many other ways very similar. We shared the same kind of background, too. His father was also in the Army and held the rank of major: a career that had taken him abroad, mostly to the Far East. Unlike me, however, Simon hadn't enjoyed a settled, secure home life. He had gone to boarding school at the age of six and usually spent half-term with his grandmother, only flying out as an unaccompanied minor in the care of the airline staff to join his parents during the longer holidays.

Once I moved in, Simon took me to meet his grandmother, who lived in the downstairs flat. She was a lovely old lady and afterwards gave Simon her verdict of me: 'That's a very high-spirited young girl.' I needed to be, to keep up with Simon. He knew everyone in Swanage, or so it seemed. If we walked down the High Street we would be waylaid time and again by his friends, invariably attractive girls. It was the same when he took me to the one and only nightclub in Swanage, a dark cellar bar attached to a hotel. We'd only be there a few minutes before some pretty girl would come over to say hello, and Simon was flirtatious with all of them. It was impossible to tell which ones were former girlfriends and which ones were applying for the post. With his experience of travelling and living abroad he seemed like something of a jetsetter in the setting of that little Dorset town and his friends were glamorous too. Often they had spent time away from Dorset and were back visiting their parents. Many had boats and sports cars. They were a well-connected and cliquey crowd whose parents invariably owned major hotels or big businesses in the area and clearly picked up many of the bills for their sons and daughters.

Even among the fast crowd, Simon was a bit of a catch, and he knew it. We had some terrible spats over his flirtatious manner but I could give as good as I got. I liked men who were highly motivated, impulsive and had an element of naughtiness about them. Simon, with his hunky physique, charm and quick mind was the first person I had been involved with who had all these things. I had always been challenging to men and now here was a man who was challenging to me. After one of these spats we would always make love with a new intensity. Sometimes our 'duels' over who was in control went unacknowledged but suddenly he would focus all his considerable charm on me and take me to a special restaurant, impressing me by ordering exotic dishes I had never tasted before.

The first three weeks passed in blissful indulgence. Simon had a date fixed for a final interview for a job as marketing executive with a computer company, but until then his time was his own. His flat in his grandmother's tall, narrow house was small but comfortable. His room was dominated by a double bed, at the foot of which stood the ornate, carved wooden rocking-horse, a relic of his childhood, that had attracted my attention on our first evening. In the tiny kitchen, Simon, who enjoyed cooking, occasionally made us a casserole. A small flight of stairs led down to a bathroom. The sitting room looked out on to the street with deep sash windows.

We discovered that we enjoyed doing the same sort of things as each other: swimming, boats, the outdoor life, and we both loved animals. We went all around the beautiful Isle of Purbeck, as that area of Dorset is known, and along the coast towards Lulworth Cove, the next bay down. Simon knew special places to go and, together with his friends, we took picnics to secret little bays and beaches only accessible by boat. He was a very strong swimmer and had won competitions for his best stroke, which was butterfly. His well-defined shoulders and muscular back gave him a strong physique I found very attractive. On other occasions we would drive out to a beautiful pub set high up in the Dorset hills with spectacular views. In the evenings, as dusk fell, we would often walk up on to a beautiful green hill overlooking Swanage and lie together in the grass. The sweetness of the summer air and the sense of comfort I always derived from the countryside was a blissful feeling. When Simon held me securely in his arms on those occasions my world felt pretty near perfect.

One weekend we went to stay with a friend of Simon's called Tony, who lived in Winchester. Tony's older sister had a boutique in Winchester High Street and he lived in a spacious flat above the shop with his girlfriend, a model. During our stay there, to make our room more romantic, Simon took the mattress off the bed and positioned it in an alcove with some bedding draped across like a curtain. It made an intimate little love nest for us – at that stage we wanted only to be in each other's arms. Although I was not on the pill, because the side effects didn't agree with me, I was quite happy that we were using condoms. Simon seemed so sophisticated, so assured at two years older than me, that I was sure nothing could go wrong.

On the day of his interview he had to travel to Farnborough by train. I waited around at the flat, killing time until he came back. It was the first day we had spent apart since meeting at the party. I was expecting him to return by train again and when I heard a car draw up outside thought it must be him in a taxi. Instead, in the street below, Simon was standing by a gleaming brand-new red Capri, smiling and giving me the thumbs-up sign. He came running upstairs, lifting me off the ground in a big hug, saying he had been in such a hurry to get back to me that he had kept driving over the pavements. He'd got the job and immediately wanted us to go out to dinner to celebrate. In the restaurant he asked me to go with him to Fareham, a small town an hour's drive away in Hampshire, where the job was. Of course I said yes. We were besotted with each other and I couldn't have been happier.

chapter six

Broken Dreams

My father put the announcement of our engagement in the *Daily Telegraph*. I didn't want him to but he was a formal man who believed in the proper way of doing things. Births, deaths and marriages, he felt, should be announced in the paper that they and most of their friends read. I was embarrassed about the announcement. It seemed such an old-fashioned way of behaving and Simon was slightly shocked. He probably felt my father was taking over. Certainly Simon had never done the old-fashioned thing and asked my father for my hand in marriage. There was something of a chasm between them. However, with the appearance of a sapphire engagement ring on my finger, my parents put whatever doubts they had about Simon behind them and welcomed him into our family. I was their only daughter and if this was the man I loved enough to marry, they were going to like him.

My mother perhaps had a harder time stifling those doubts than my father. In the intuitive way mothers often have about their daughter's lives, she worried about the arrogance that was an integral part of Simon's personality. She also felt, with my abrupt departure from the family home, that he had somehow taken me away.

'Why do you have to live with him? Just see him at weekends,' was her constant advice while I was in Swanage, and when she heard of our decision to set up home together in Fareham she became even more anxious, going so far as to say, 'Living together like that won't work.' Mine was the first generation to openly live together without marrying and it was so utterly alien to her. It seemed risky to the point of danger.

For me, however, the sense of adventure and risk was part of the main attraction. Simon found a little bungalow to rent in Fareham, the small town adjacent to Gosport in Hampshire where his new job was based. It was comfortable enough, in a rented accommodation sort of way, but then if he had invited me to go and live in a hole in the ground with him I probably would have. The passion of our love affair was all-consuming; domestic matters were not high on my agenda.

His office was at one end of the High Street and I got a secretarial job with a firm of solicitors whose offices were at the other end. Each morning we would leave the bungalow together: Simon in a suit complete with kipper tie, me in flares and platform boots. We were so besotted with each other that after we'd said goodbye in the morning we often used to ring each other almost as soon as we got into work. When we could, we met for lunch in our favourite wine bar.

In the evenings when we went out to dinner in restaurants, which we did often, we began to plot our future. Simon had travelled extensively, often flying out to spend holidays with his parents often in the Far East. The experience made him think way beyond the confines of sleepy Fareham and he talked of the opportunities that existed in Hong Kong where he had contacts. He also talked of our life as a couple.

'When we get married I'd love you to have a child. I want you to have a little boy and he'll look just like me,' Simon told me one evening over dinner. His words thrilled me and, at the time, I didn't see that this was a wish tinged with perhaps more than a little egocentricity. But then, his whole life had been about managing on his own. Simon's parents were still abroad so I never met them and he rarely mentioned them. Although his granny lived in Swanage he didn't seem to have a close relationship with her either. He probably found it odd and even a little irritating that my own parents were so interested and wanted to be so closely involved in my life. As far as I was concerned, however, Simon was my life. He was a terrifically good-looking man with a lot of attitude and drive. I believed in him and our future together one hundred per cent.

At the end of our first month together, I took him to see my old school. We'd both shared stories of the awful life at boarding school; it was another thing we had in common. I hadn't been back to Leweston since I was 16, and was struck by what a beautiful setting it was. I especially remembered a long avenue of grass which ended in a paved viewing area with a stone balustrade around it. It was known as the Belvedere and one of my daydreams had been to imagine myself getting married and walking down that beautiful natural aisle as a bride. When I was at the school, old girls had often come back and the nuns always loved to hear what had happened in their lives, so Simon and I knocked at the door. Sure enough they made us very welcome and insisted we came in to have tea with them. I told them we were engaged and they were delighted and asked, 'Have you known each other long?' Without blinking Simon said, 'Four months.' Their faces immediately registered concern. 'Oh, not very long then,' they suggested politely. If they'd known it was really four weeks I'm sure I would have featured in their prayers that night.

There was no doubt that we were having a lot of fun together. Our shared natural optimism made us able to enjoy the moment. One weekend a big fair set up on the outskirts of the town. I especially loved fairgrounds; the rides, the atmosphere, the excitement. We spent the evening eating candyfloss and hot dogs and going on all the fastest rides. When we began to feel as though everything was spinning even with our feet on the ground, we staggered back to the bungalow. Once home, though, I had that terrible feeling that went beyond feeling queasy, I thought I might actually *be* sick. I was just holding on to the side of the bath and trying to exercise mind over the matter of my stomach when the bathroom door burst open and suddenly Simon and I were vomiting into each end of the bath. How romantic is that? Later, that terrible image made us laugh.

Another weekend we drove down to Bath to visit friends of mine for the day. Jo Hart, who had shared so many escapades with me at school and with whom I'd rented my first flat in Bournemouth, had trained as a nurse and met and married a doctor. They were living in hospital accommodation in a complex which had a swimming pool. I had met so many of Simon's friends and I was proud to introduce him to mine. Simon was very charming and made a good impression on Jo, who later told me what a dishy guy she thought he was. It was a lovely day and Simon went swimming before we drove back to Fareham in the Capri.

It was some months after we'd set up home together that I realised I'd missed a period. I felt a slight twinge of anxiety but the idea I could be pregnant seemed impossible and I pushed it to the back of my mind. It wasn't until about ten days later that I suddenly felt a wave of nausea as I was brushing my teeth, and the anxiety I was trying to suppress could no longer be ignored.

I came back into the bedroom where Simon was buttoning his shirt and searching for a tie at the same time.

'I just felt incredibly sick,' I told him.

'Is it a bug? Maybe it's the prawns we had last night,' he said.

'And my period's late. Very late,' I said and it was as though I was acknowledging these things to myself for the first time. As I spoke, Simon had got down to search for one of his shoes that was lodged under the bed. At my words he seemed to freeze, then slowly his face appeared on the other side of the bed.

'Do you think you're pregnant?' His tone was neutral but his face was clouded with anxiety. I felt a rush of relief that he cared so much about me.

'No, I think it's those prawns,' I reassured him, but as I began to work out in my head just how overdue my period was, I felt doubtful.

We didn't say anything else about it, but on several occasions over the next week I noticed Simon looking intently at me when I came back from the bathroom as though he was hoping I'd say something. I had another bout of feeling mildly sick on the way to work one morning. Could I really be pregnant? I was worried but kept dismissing the idea. The fears I felt were also tempered by the memory of the wonderful words Simon had said months earlier. After all, we had our lives planned out and even if I was pregnant – which at that stage I couldn't really imagine I was – it was something we could cope with together. When more than three weeks had passed with no sign of a period I forced myself to stop burying my head in the sand and get a pregnancy test done at the doctor's. I had to phone for the result. 'Yes, it is positive,' the clinic nurse told me cheerfully. Until that moment the possibility that I actually was pregnant had seemed completely unreal. Babies were something that *other* people, grown-up people, had. I was shocked but the thought came from the back of my mind to comfort me and stop me plunging into a total state of horror: this was what Simon wanted anyway. He had said he'd love me to have a child and, I thought, so what if it was something that was happening a little ahead of schedule? We'd cope. We were madly in love, planning to marry and I knew we would adore our baby and be devoted parents.

I called Simon at work and he asked immediately: 'What was the result?' I told him and he made a very brief response, but I knew that was to be expected as he was in the office and couldn't speak. That afternoon my thoughts raced ahead. I began to feel twinges of excitement as the news sank in. Would it be a little boy and really look like Simon, as he'd said? I put my hand on my stomach. That there was a baby on the way seemed terrifying and wonderful at the same time.

That night we went out for a meal. After we had ordered pasta, Simon looked directly at me across the table: 'I think it would be best if you had an abortion.' At first I didn't think I'd heard him right. I just stared at him, saying, 'What?' and then when he repeated it I managed to ask, 'Why?' Waiters began to put food on the table and Simon poured us both a glass of wine. I couldn't move. I simply sat and stared at him as tears began trickling down my face.

'I thought you wanted to marry me and for us to have a child,' I managed to choke out.

'I do, but please understand, I don't want you to have a baby just yet. I've got to get my career established. It just isn't the right time.'

How we finished the meal, paid the bill and left the restaurant I have no memory. I simply couldn't believe he'd even uttered the word 'abortion'. It wasn't my Catholic upbringing that made it so abhorrent, I could just never imagine feeling it was something I would go ahead with, I thought then and still believe that women should have the right to make their own choice. It was simply that this was our baby and I knew it was right that this baby should be born.

The next couple of weeks were terrible. Simon begged and pleaded with me to change my mind and have an abortion. Just hearing how insistent he was would reduce me to tears instantly. I seemed always to be crying. His lack of immediate family meant that now, in his twenties, he was a very free agent. There were no constraints at all on him and he behaved just as he pleased. He'd had to learn to become independent at an early age, which perhaps gave him the hard edge I was beginning to see. I was devastated by his attitude but I had no one to talk to. I knew if my parents got involved they would be hugely protective of me and naturally against him. It would turn nasty and become a war between Simon and my family... and of course I still loved him so much. I spoke to my mother regularly on the phone and although I made a huge effort to sound casual her antennae were at full stretch. 'Is something wrong?' she began to ask. 'Why don't you just come home for a bit?' I had to tell my boss at work a little of what was happening and he was very supportive and kind. It was apparent something was terribly wrong and although I tried hard to put it out of my mind in the office, in truth I thought of nothing else.

For his part, Simon took the traditional masculine route when faced with an intractable problem: avoidance. He loved rugby and had played all his life. When we moved to Fareham he had joined the local club and when things were going well between us I was happy for him to go to practices and even went along to watch a match or two. Simon's energy and impressive physique were all part of his appeal. Now, however, the rugby club and a ready supply of drinking friends provided a handy escape from a problem he couldn't handle. Increasingly, when I came back to the bungalow at the end of the day, he had gone straight from work to play rugby. He began staying late at the club, drinking afterwards and only arriving back home towards midnight. I was so lonely, so desperate, rattling around in that bungalow with a hundred thoughts churning around in my mind.

Things got so bad that he even began going out without me at weekends and didn't bother to make excuses. I retaliated by going home to spend the weekends with my parents in Blandford. A chasm was opening between us. Suddenly, Simon announced that he had bought me a car. It was a second-hand Hillman Imp and he said it was a present so I could get around without relying on him to drive me. It was obviously bought in the hope of winning me back. I hated it immediately. In my mind it seemed to stand for some sort of bribery and the question of our baby was so much bigger than that.

All the time the weeks were passing and the question of whether a termination would even be possible was becoming slimmer. In what was almost certainly desperation Simon finally came up with a suggestion: 'Let's go and see the doctor and he can help us sort it out,' he said. I think he imagined the doctor would see there was only one possible solution to this problem.

He made an appointment at the practice in Fareham where I'd had the pregnancy test. When my name was called we both went in and, sitting side by side, Simon began to explain the dilemma. He said the pregnancy was an accident, that it had happened at the wrong time and a termination was the sensible option for us both in the long run. Hearing him say all this started the tears flowing again and I was pretty incoherent. To Simon's huge amazement the doctor turned to him and said:

'I think it would be better if you waited outside while I talk to Fiona.'

When Simon began to protest the doctor said, 'You, young man, are very arrogant,' and practically ordered him out of the surgery. Simon was annoyed and totally surprised but in the end he had no option but to go to the waiting room.

'Now,' said the doctor turning to me, 'what do you want to do?'

'I want to have this baby,' I managed to say.

'Well, you shall,' he said. Just hearing him say that was suddenly such a tremendous relief. He made it sound so simple. After weeks of misery it was as though at least one thing was definite. I felt that surely Simon would accept what the doctor said... after all, he'd suggested we went to see him.

I was so wrong. When I told him in the car that the doctor had said I should go ahead and that was what I was going to do, he fell completely silent. Back at the bungalow he began trying once more to coax me into changing my mind. When I said I had firmly made up my mind to go ahead he replied that if that was the case I had to go home. We had always been stubborn people, challenging each other in silly flirtatious ways, but now this was a huge adult decision. Neither of us would back down and Simon played the ultimate card: 'If you go ahead and have this baby, I will not marry you.'

Simon simply didn't understand how I had begun to feel for the baby growing inside me; the baby I had increasingly begun to think of as my baby. I knew I would be alone and lonely as a single mother and I was frightened by that. At the same time I felt so protective towards my unborn baby and my feelings towards Simon began to change. How could a man be so cruel? I began to think I'd made a huge mistake and that perhaps he wasn't the man I'd thought he was. The doctor's simple words of affirmation had made me stronger.

'I'm having this baby; you are not going to change my mind,' I told him.

By now my mother had guessed what was happening and she began calling me, urging me towards home and security. For my part I was trying to delay the terrible moment when I would walk away from Simon, hoping against hope we could sort it out together.

When I realised the time had come that I had to go home, I was so desperately hurt.

I was going home with my tail between my legs. All my brave breaking of rules had ended in disaster, just as my mother had predicted. It was an awful moment. Simon drove me back to Blandford – I refused to have anything to do with the hated Hillman

Imp and left it sitting outside the bungalow. When we arrived he simply dropped me at the gate because he was too scared to see my parents. I walked back into the kitchen, alone, with my suitcase in my hand. I was three months pregnant.

chapter seven
Tough Decisions

Every time the phone went, the post arrived or I heard the sound of a car pulling up outside the house, Simon's face sprang into my mind. I simply couldn't believe he would abandon me and our baby so completely and finally. I alternated between a numb misery that he could be so cold and cruel as to dump me on the doorstep, and an equally desperate hope that he would come and get me. I thought about him all the time. I wrote, pleading with him not to abandon me. I was madly in love, despite his cruel treatment, and pined for him every minute.

My mother's way of coping was to put on a very businesslike front. She tried to comfort me by saying, 'You've done the right thing at last. Now don't have anything else to do with him.' But because I still loved him I didn't want to hear anything bad about him, even though he was behaving so terribly. My father was more conciliatory. In such an emotional state little things acted as triggers, sending me rushing upstairs to my bedroom in floods of tears, slamming the door behind me. I was very up and down. My mother's answer was to blot out all talk or thoughts about 'that creature'. I'd been very silly and got myself into the kind of mess she had predicted but never mind, she and my father were there for me and they'd look after me.

Although her words about Simon were brisk and it was not in her nature to talk about emotions, she did everything she could physically to soothe the hurt. When I was a child she'd always spoiled me, and now she loved to do the same. She was a natural homemaker and wanted to cosset and look after us all. Every morning she came into my bedroom, drawing back the curtains, and asked me what I wanted for breakfast. Toast, porridge or a boiled egg? Then I'd hear her downstairs in the kitchen, cupboard doors opening and shutting, the kettle boiling. Soon her steps sounded on the stairs again and there was the rattle of a breakfast tray, all beautifully laid out, which she set down on my bedside table. She cared about me so much and to her it was best to write Simon out of my life completely.

Despite the love my parents surrounded me with, at first I became quite depressed. I couldn't explain the emotions I was going through. Then, when I got to six months and my expanding stomach could no longer be concealed beneath baggy sweaters, I began to feel horribly embarrassed and humiliated. Our family home was an environment where sex was never mentioned. If something of a vaguely sexual nature came on the television my mother would immediately switch it off, saying, 'We're not going to have that sort of thing in *this* house.' Yet here I was, with the proof of my scandalous love life becoming more obvious by the day. My two brothers were living at home at that stage, and that added to my constant embarrassment. It was all so horribly wrong. I should have been sharing this experience with a lovely husband. Instead I felt shame and degradation.

The worst days were Sundays. My parents were devout Catholics and it was expected that we would all go and take Holy Communion at the local church. My father also played the organ every Sunday at our church. There was simply no question of not going. Each week I had to make a spectacle of myself waddling up the aisle behind my mother and father, my huge bump becoming increasingly obvious. Of course everybody in the church knew what had happened. I simply wouldn't speak or look at anybody. As the weeks went by I got larger and larger and at eight months I was so big I had to go for a special scan as they thought it might be twins. Not for the first time I imagined I might be the subject of a few people's prayers for forgiveness.

Outside the house I felt isolated. I went to a few antenatal classes but I hated them because all the other mothers were married and the inevitable questions came up, 'What does your husband do?' and 'Is he going to be at the birth?' I was so ashamed of my situation.

*   *   *

As autumn turned to winter and decorations and lights began to appear in the shop windows, I still couldn't believe Simon wouldn't come for me. Christmas was especially painful. To protect myself from the loneliness I began to focus more on my baby. I was convinced from the earliest days that it was a HE and decided early on he was going to be called Duncan, a name I'd heard and liked. My parents were delighted because we've all got Scottish names. The idea that I was going to meet someone who was my own flesh and blood for the first time was also very much with me during the pregnancy. That was how I got through all that humiliation. I was going to have this baby and it was part of me. Long before the birth I had bonded with him very strongly and however alone I felt, I never regretted my decision. This baby was going to be something very, very special. It was him and me.

In the last months my slim figure totally disappeared as I sought consolation in food. Doughnuts were my particular weakness and I ate not just one but often two or even three at a time. I put on three and a half stone in weight and didn't care.

I was slightly in denial about the actual birth and hadn't really any idea what to expect. When I got to eight months I just wanted it to be born and was thankful he arrived a few days early, even though it meant a mad dash to hospital in the middle of the night. My parents must have been so anxious as they waited those long hours from our arrival at the hospital at 2am until 5am when the midwife finally brought them the news they had been longing to hear. I don't know what was going through my mother's mind when she and my father were finally ushered into my room as dawn began to break on 7 April 1979. However, as soon as they looked at that tiny baby, Duncan, less than an hour old in his little cot, I saw only love on their faces. It must have been an emotional moment on many levels. My mother had never experienced a successful birth, but she did not reveal her deeper feelings. They remained secret from me, and maybe from herself too.

They finally went home at 9am and I was transferred to a small ward with three other mothers. I was much too excited to sleep and just kept staring at my perfect baby beside me. The following day a doctor came round to examine me and, with a group of medical students all standing at the foot of the bed peering down, told them I had needed internal and external stitches and that this was a classic case of tearing. He never spoke directly to me at all. I was shocked and upset because, in so many ways, I was such a modest girl. My parents were almost verging on prudish, the nuns in the convent had encouraged modesty and I had been brought up in that way. I wanted to get up and go home immediately. Instead I had to spend ten long days there. The stitches meant it was agony to walk when the nurses first helped me out of bed, but I wasn't alone in that experience. We all used to take cushions with us to sit at the table for our meals. No one asked me about my husband, I was just another mother in hospital with a baby, but they must have thought it strange that no man came to visit me. I had visits from my brothers and parents, but no one single man.

Three days after Duncan's birth the sister came to tell me, 'You've got a phone call, it's Charles.' I said I didn't know anyone of that name but I went to the phone and as soon as I heard a familiar voice say 'Hello Fiona' a jolt of adrenalin surged through me. It was Simon. He had given a false name because he knew that otherwise I wouldn't speak to him.

'I had a feeling you might have produced by now,' he said. 'Is it a boy or a girl?'

I was so shocked I just automatically replied: 'It's a boy.'

'I told you, didn't I, it would be a boy?' he said. He started to say something else but I put the phone down and burst into tears. All the feelings of loneliness I had been trying to suppress flooded back. I didn't want to go back to the ward and face questions. Instead I crept off and sobbed my heart out in the toilets. When my father came that evening he was angry to hear what had happened. Unbeknown to me he had secretly given instructions that I was not to receive any outside phone calls because he wanted to protect me at such a vulnerable time.

When I came home from the hospital the season seemed to have turned to spring overnight and the hedgerows and gardens were alive with the cheering vibrant yellow of daffodils. With the arrival of the baby my mother's attitude also changed completely. In a way having the baby made everything all right between us once more. I had given her this lovely being she could pour love into and she was overjoyed. I was no longer the bad girl.

I had a good feeling about life. It was a relief not to be so huge any more and my parents made me feel very secure. They cushioned me from the harsh realities of life. I was tired and felt both emotionally and physically drained and I was happy for my mother, who was brilliant with babies, to take over. The baby's cot was in my small bedroom and in those first weeks it felt like my own little domain, my territory. After hospital life it was also lovely to have my own things around me. I was a bit apprehensive that Duncan might keep me awake all night. In hospital the nurses had given him a bottle at night, but back at home I was lucky and he slept peacefully.

It was a happy, exciting time. My parents were overjoyed with the baby and I couldn't wait to put him in a pram and take him for a walk – a thing I'd seen other people do. Now it was my turn. I shared all this pleasure and enjoyment with my mother who was naturally a big influence on me. I knew nothing about babies and I hadn't even held a baby before, as none of my friends or relatives had babies. My mother was a great believer that babies needed fresh air and loved taking him for walks. 'Babies need to get out every day,' she said and I followed her lead.

To my parents it was obvious that Simon was not going to accept responsibility for Duncan or for me. My own feelings were much less clear. I still loved Simon, in fact I was still obsessed with him and thought of him all the time. It was painful to face the harsh fact that he wanted nothing to do with me or our baby. I was happy for my father, who saw it as his role to 'sort things out', to take over. His sense of decency was outraged by Simon's behaviour and his first impulse was to write, man to man, to Simon's father to try to get Simon to own up to his responsibilities.

Simon's parents had rented their home out to the local bank manager while they were away but my father wrote a letter to their home address in the belief that mail would be forwarded. My father felt that Simon's father should be aware of the situation if he was not already. They were both army men and should live by the same code of conduct. When he didn't receive a reply he was amazed. I don't know if the letter was intercepted by Simon or whether his parents at that stage knew the facts about our relationship or, indeed, if they even knew they had a grandson. Simon had a determined personality and he may have told them he wasn't the father or that this was a fantasy on the part of a girl who was obsessed with him. It would be natural for parents to want to believe their son.

When nothing was forthcoming my father said, 'Like father, like son,' and reluctantly took the step of consulting a lawyer. A paternity suit was issued and the legal documents were again delivered to Simon at his parents' address. By this time we heard they had come back to Swanage. The court case was scheduled for a month after Duncan's birth, in May. My mother stayed at home looking after Duncan and my father and I went together to the preliminary hearing, which was held in the Corn Exchange in Blandford. We met our solicitor there and he led us up some narrow, rickety steps to wait outside the courtroom until it was our turn. As I was standing beside my father I turned and saw Simon arrive with his solicitor. I had known he would be there but it was still a shock. I felt unexpectedly trembly and my throat tightened. I was glad we were called quickly and filed into what really resembled a room rather than a formal court. Our solicitor set out the details of the case and then Simon's solicitor said he was contesting paternity and requested a blood test. I didn't think I was hearing him correctly for a minute. How could Simon deny our relationship? More horrible still was the insinuation that the father of my baby could have been any one of a number of men. My father squeezed my arm in support but I couldn't control my tears. I didn't look at Simon.

A date was set for the following week when myself, Simon and the baby all had to go to Dorchester Hospital for a blood test. The samples had to be taken on the same day. I just felt numb. Then we all filed out of the court. As I emerged on to the little landing at the top of the stairs I glanced through an open door and saw Simon standing with his solicitor. He was smirking. My father was wonderful and, putting a protective arm around me, shepherded me past them and out into the street. He felt so much for me, but this was something he couldn't magically make right.

In all the scenarios I had imagined between Simon and me, most of them centring on us somehow getting back together, I had never imagined he would try to deny that Duncan was his baby. I don't know why he did that. I don't know why he did any of it. Perhaps he thought I wouldn't go through with a test or perhaps he was playing for time. On the day in question my father drove me and my mother, who came to help with Duncan, to Dorchester Hospital. We checked in with the nurse and joined the other people waiting for blood tests. Opposite was a woman with a teenage daughter who talked about glandular fever. Most of the other people were elderly. I wondered what they would think if they knew the purpose behind our test. All the time I was tense, and I could tell my parents were too, in case Simon appeared. In the event we had the test, which made Duncan howl briefly, and got clear of the hospital without seeing any sign of him. I was relieved.

The next thing we heard, via our solicitor, was that Simon didn't even show up at the hospital. The matter was referred back to the court, although this time we didn't need to attend, and a ruling was made in my favour with an order for Simon to pay maintenance for Duncan. I was glad it was finally settled. Then two days later I answered the phone one morning at home and it was Simon on the line. He said he was calling from Hong Kong, that he'd gone out there to work and live and wouldn't be paying maintenance. I listened, practically in silence, and then put the phone down. What was there to say? My father was outraged that

Simon could just walk away without accepting any responsibility at all. He had some connections in Hong Kong and wrote to the authorities out there with details of the court order. Eventually he received a reply saying the order was only enforceable if Simon was in the United Kingdom. While in Hong Kong he was outside British jurisdiction and nothing could touch him. At that point my father had to admit defeat and Simon Roscoe went out of my life, though not out of my mind, for many years.

chapter eight

Natural Born Charmer

From Duncan's earliest days music was part of his life. My father was the source of this, either playing records or sitting down at the magnificent Beckstein grand piano which dominated our modest sitting room. As a teenager I remember my father's excitement when that grand piano arrived. He'd found it rotting away in one of the storerooms at Blandford Camp, where he was stationed, and had been able to buy it cheaply and have it restored. After Sunday lunch I would join my father and play duets with him.

Duncan's early childhood was a mix of the traditions of the fifties, from my mother's ways, and the seventies from things he did with me. There was no discord between my mother and I over who did what as Duncan grew from a baby to a toddler. She loved to fuss over him and had endless patience, particularly during the baby and toddler stages. He grew up enjoying the same warmth, love and secure routines that had been part of my childhood; home-cooked meals, church on Sunday followed by a traditional family lunch. I took care of everything that happened outside the home: outings, friendships and later school. Nor was there any confusion in Duncan's mind over our roles; he especially idolised my mother but he called my parents Grandma and Grandpa and I was always Mummy. When he got older he did two cards on Mother's Day, one for me and another with 'Grandma' written on the front.

My parents' house was in the centre of Blandford and as soon as Duncan could walk well enough we made regular outings together. He was a very good walker early on, partly because I tended to walk everywhere with him rather than take a pushchair. He would just put his hand in mine, and off we'd go. Often it was to the ducks or on a shopping errand into town. Sometimes we went further afield. I had a bicycle with a little seat on the back and in summer I used to take him to a farm outside the town where you could pick your own strawberries.

Duncan's personality was apparent early on. He was charming, sensitive and, for a young child, had an intuitiveness that people readily responded to. These natural traits were probably accentuated by living in a house with three adults who didn't talk down to him, but from when he was two or three years old he had something special about him, a natural charm and the most lovely manners. We couldn't go into town without having to stop and talk all the time to people, shop-keepers and friends of my parents and even complete strangers, who always ended up saying, 'He's such a credit to you.'

One of the places we regularly called on during our shopping rounds was an old-fashioned butchers which my mother had used ever since they moved to Blandford. The butcher, Mr Peaple, was a big, rather austere man who wore the full butcher's regalia of straw hat and blue-and-white-striped butchers apron over his white overall. He was a very pleasant man but he was also rather intimidating, even I was a little bit in awe of him. He knew all our family and during my pregnancy would always talk to me when I came in to collect the meat.

He treated Duncan like a miniature adult. When Duncan came in holding my hand, Mr Peaple looked down at him and said: 'And how are you today, Master Duncan?' in his booming voice. Duncan didn't hide behind me or stare at the ground, like many small children would have. He looked right back up and said: 'I'm very well, thank you, and how are you?' Everyone was always won over by such charming manners from a tiny child.

Duncan loved going out and he was always very interested in people, whatever their age. Some children tend to respond mainly to other children but he was just as chatty to adults. When we walked into town there was one old man who always spoke to us because he enjoyed talking to Duncan, who called him 'my friend'. Duncan would spot him before I did and say, 'Look Mummy, there's my friend.' We would cross over the road and the old man's eyes would light up and they would chat. Duncan never forgot a face. This went on for years. The old man would always give Duncan a sweet (although in fact savoury things like crisps were Duncan's favourites), remember his birthday and put a card through our letterbox.

I shied away from going to 'mother and toddler' clubs. I suppose I didn't feel part of the world the other mothers there all shared. Often they had a second baby or were pregnant again, and married usually, and their lives seemed mapped out. My own future was so uncertain. It was hard to get involved in their conversations.

At home, however, there was a lot of happiness. Having a young child around the house was a continual source of delight to my parents and sharing that made us very close. My mother liked to spoil him, just as she did me. When we came in from shopping or a trip to see the ducks she made him a cup of tea and brought him toast or a sandwich with it and put it on a little round brass table we had in front of the television. Watching *Playschool* was a daily treat and *Rainbow*, with Zippy and Bungle, was another big hit.

Duncan never ever asked about his father in any detail. I was always waiting for the day when he would ask me where Simon was but it never came. He just accepted the fact that he didn't have a father. If something arose that entailed having a dad to join in he'd just say in a matter-of-fact way, 'I can't do that because I haven't got a father.' He always knew Simon's name and no doubt absorbed a good deal of my mother's attitude: 'We don't want to talk about *that* creature.' He took his lead from her, probably, and wanted to be supportive and protective of me. And hopefully he felt he had all the love and care he needed at home with us.

Gradually I began to pick up the threads of my life again. My mother was very generous about baby-sitting although, to be truthful, she and my father rarely went out in any case. Her only stipulation was that she preferred Duncan to be in bed and asleep before I left. This was easier said than done because by the time he was approaching his second birthday he'd developed the most acute antennae, picking up any clues that I might be going out. It wasn't that he minded being left with Grandma, it was all about trying to control the situation. He clearly didn't think I should be going out without him. His cot was still in my bedroom and in order to get him to go to sleep I had to resort to lying down on my bed and pretending I was going to sleep as well. I made my breathing very regular and lay perfectly still, listening for his breathing to follow suit. It often took as long as an hour before, very cautiously, I could get up and begin to creep towards the door. Quite often, just as I thought I'd made it safely away, a little voice would suddenly pipe up: 'Where are you going?' I'd have to make up a hasty excuse, get back on the bed and start all over again. On at least one occasion it took so long I fell asleep myself.

I didn't have a huge circle of friends in Blandford, because I'd always been away at boarding school, but I was very sociable and as I got my confidence back I began to meet new people. By now my chances of meeting the right man had become infinitely more complicated. I always told men I went out with about Duncan. I was proud of him for one thing, and having a little boy was a big part of my life. I have also always been a very honest, direct person and decided that if it was any problem to them that I had a child, then they weren't the kind of people I wanted to know.

I met a man named James at a party. He was eight years older than me and was very keen. Soon we began going out regularly. My parents liked him a lot; he had his own house in Poole, a good job as an electrical engineer, and was lovely with Duncan, who was almost two at the time. It may have been because of some unspoken pressure from everyone who saw James as the perfect husband for me and a father for Duncan, but when he proposed marriage I accepted, even though in my heart I knew my feelings for him weren't tinged with the same passion I had felt for Simon. My parents were naturally delighted and James said that when we were married he wanted to adopt Duncan. Plans began to steam ahead for the wedding. My mother came with me to buy the wedding dress and soon we were counting down the weeks to the big day. But my secret doubts began to mount. I tried to convince myself that I was making the right decision but I felt increasingly anxious. Finally I blurted out to my mother: 'I can't go through with it. I don't love him.' Of all the many, many tests her difficult daughter had confronted her with this must have been one of the hardest, but to her eternal credit she didn't fly into a panic or try to put any pressure on me. Instead she said quite calmly, 'Well, why should you settle for second best?'

I owed it to James to tell him face to face. It was one of the hardest things I'd ever had to do because he was so kind, so decent. He was devastated. 'You would grow to love me,' he said when I explained why I couldn't go ahead. But somehow I knew it would never work out if we started from such a base. Maybe that was selfish of me, because it would have given Duncan a more conventional childhood.

After that I decided to apply to train as a nurse. I had a child to support and knew I couldn't lean on my parents forever. I had always felt an instinctive empathy with anyone vulnerable and my experiences over the last couple of years had heightened that. My mother was very encouraging and she and my father said they would happily look after Duncan while I was at work, so I knew he would be secure and happy. I applied to Poole Hospital and was accepted just as Duncan was coming up to two. I had to sleep over when I was on night shifts, otherwise I commuted from my parents' house.

The training turned out to be a mixed bag of experiences. Some aspects I found hard. The strict hierarchy was so like school and the petty regulations and bureaucracy were never to do with the real care of the patients. One or two senior staff made it their business to take it out on trainee nurses. My most enjoyable placement was in the geriatric ward. I found I loved working with old people. They had all led such interesting lives. Most were born in the previous century and had been through two world wars. They would tell me their stories and I took time to listen. Through this I came to know them as individuals, and imagine them as young men and women. I found old people rewarding, not demanding. By contrast my most testing time was in the orthopaedic ward. There was very little nursing to do, time being the great healer there, and a lot of technical equipment to master – all those pulleys and hoists to manoeuvre.

I made some friends among the other nurses but one day, walking down one of the long corridors, I caught a glimpse of a familiar face flashing past. I thought she seemed to glance at me and it took a few minutes to register that it was Helen Vallie. For some strange reason, because we didn't say hello immediately, we never did acknowledge each other all the time we were there. I discovered she had started a year ahead of me and was a second-year nurse. For my part I was embarrassed because of all the events that had stemmed from that night at her 21st birthday. I wasn't sure how much she knew. On her side, she was probably equally unsure what to say. We solved the problem by simply behaving as if we didn't know the other was there.

I qualified as a nurse in the same year that Duncan started

school. Where to send him was an easy decision as my father was by now a teacher at a boys' prep school. He had retired from the Army when he was 55, in the same year I left school, and had taken a teaching job at Dumpton Prep School, where he became the deputy headmaster and taught French and music. The main part of the school was in a beautiful old house surrounded by lovely grounds in a village near Wimborne. It was a small, friendly school whose motto was: 'You can because you think you can.' My parents offered to help with the fees, which were reduced because my father taught there, and I gratefully accepted. My nurse's salary wouldn't have stretched that far and there was no other source of income for Duncan. When I took him up on his first day at the pre-prep school, Duncan looked absurdly small, dwarfed by the blazer which had been bought with room for him to grow into. He took to school immediately and my father or I would drive him there each morning.

I still didn't fit in easily with the other mothers. Maybe it was my imagination, but being a single mother in the seventies seemed to have a big stigma attached to it and that did affect my personality, making me more withdrawn. Despite my parents being so loving and supportive I also felt embarrassed for them and felt their friends must think it was terrible that I was living at home with a baby and no husband. However, there were one or two kindred spirits I got on with. Sheila Geary, who had a little boy called Stephen, became a good friend. For whatever reason, she wasn't into the young mums' scene either, and I used to go round to her house for coffee while our sons played together. Soon after we met we were in her house chatting when I thought I heard a 'miaow' coming from her garage. Her cat had had kittens and she had one left from the litter that she couldn't find a home for. That teatime Duncan and I arrived back at my parents' house with a large cardboard box. What was inside grew into the sweetest little cat who we called Suki, who lived to the amazing age of 24.

As Duncan got older my parents took to hiring a beach hut at Bournemouth for two weeks in the summer. It wasn't far to drive for a day out and the hut had a little cooker, so we could make cups of tea or simple meals. At the start of the two weeks we'd fill the hut with all Duncan's bucket-and-spade gear and our deckchairs. My father's concession to these seaside outings was to take off his jacket . He sat in a deckchair on the little veranda of the beach hut wearing a collar and tie, reading his paper and puffing his pipe.

Duncan still hadn't lost the knack of striking up conversations with adults he took a shine to and it was on one of our trips to Bournemouth that he collected another 'friend'. This time it was a lady in her sixties who obviously lived nearby and, to judge by her tan and the regularity with which we encountered her, spent a lot of time on the beach. Duncan started talking to her when he sat down beside her one day on a wall by the sea's edge. Ever after, a trip to the beach meant he always looked for her and would invariably exclaim, 'Oh, there's my friend!' and take himself off to sit with her and chat.

When Duncan was nine he left Dumpton and went to Blandford Middle School for three years. He made the switch very easily and began to make more friends in the town. One of these was a girl called Tracy who was about two years older than him and lived a few doors down from my parents. He developed a huge crush on her, partly because at 11 she seemed so much more grown-up and glamorous. He watched for her out of the window in my parents' front room and when he saw her go past, walking her Jack Russell terrier, he'd nip outside to say hello. After a while she invited him to go on these walks with her. That went on for nearly three years and they're still friends to this day.

Another friend of Duncan's was a boy everyone called BJ, although his real name was Robert. He was quite a mischievous little boy and lived opposite my parents. He and Duncan went to Blandford Middle School together and under his influence Duncan got up to all sorts of naughtiness. BJ would wind him up with a daring idea but invariably it was Duncan who would actually carry out whatever deed they were plotting while BJ hung back. He and BJ had two 'girlfriends' who, I later discovered, used to hide under the desks in the classroom to kiss them. BJ's advice, Duncan told me years later, was that to kiss properly you had to pretend to be a cow chewing grass.

I used to take Duncan up to Bryanstone for piano lessons,

though like me he was lazy about practising. Part of the problem was that he had such a good ear he could pretty well reproduce a tune without learning to read the notes. The first time I realised just how talented he was, we had been on a holiday to the Isle of Wight. We went to visit the waxworks museum and Duncan was both terrified and enthralled by the Dungeons of Doom where Bach's *Sonata in D Minor*, the classic dramatic chords, sounded as you stepped inside. When we got home he was messing around on the piano and suddenly I heard him reproduce exactly those same chords that he had heard in the museum. Soon after I bought him an electronic keyboard for his tenth birthday and he used to mess around writing and composing songs. One he made up, called 'Summer Days Are Over', was so good he was asked to play it at the school assembly.

After I qualified as a nurse I took a job as a theatre nurse in an eye hospital in Bournemouth, where I stayed for 18 months. It was interesting work, although the hours were very long and I had to rely on my mother to care for Duncan after school. A spell of agency nursing followed, until I heard of a job going that suited my need to balance work and motherhood. Bryanstone School, the very same place that had been the focus of so much of my interest as a young teenager, needed a school nurse. The location was ideal, on the edge of Blandford, and I was able to take a rented house in the town for Duncan and me. The school had a sanatorium where we nursed sick pupils and ran a doctor's surgery every morning with a visiting GP from the town. The school needed 24-hour cover so the job was split into shifts which I shared with another nurse. When I had to stay overnight, Duncan was able to go back and spend the night at my parents' house where he still had his own room. It was an ideal arrangement, giving my parents a bit of much-needed space as although they adored Duncan, he was now a typically lively, fast-growing boy and often pretty noisy. It also gave Duncan and I time to be alone together.

They were very enjoyable years. As a single mother I was so lucky to have the back-up of my parents and I enjoyed my job. However, as I moved into my thirties I began to feel the lack of any kind of challenge in my life. I had always loved the countryside and animals and I felt I had skills and abilities that had never been put to the test. One evening when I was out with friends I was introduced to a man who felt just the same. Derek had been divorced once and then widowed when his second wife died in an accident. He was older than me, with grown-up children, but as we talked we found we had much in common. He had worked for years in the marine business and travelled extensively as part of his job but he was also at a stage, in his forties, where he was looking for a fresh challenge. Like me he loved the countryside and animals and had thought about setting up his own business.

It wasn't a passionate love affair, rather we were two people slightly adrift in life and we connected. Derek would say: 'Stick with me and you'll be all right.' He'd put his arm around me as he said that, which felt good. I wanted security and I knew he could give it to me. More than that, Derek wanted to give me that security. We also shared a desire for the same kind of lifestyle and began to plan and dream. I was filled with optimism about a new life for Duncan and me as we started to look for the right kind of business opportunity.

Derek and I bought a house in a village called Charlton Marshall just outside Blandford and we set up home together. Not long after we moved in he bought me a wonderful pedigree Main Coon kitten. Main Coons are one of the largest domestic cats, with a muscular body, a very dense shaggy coat and the temperament of a gentle giant. Ours was blue and white, though they are most commonly tabby, and we called him Dakar. He grew to be a truly magnificent beast.

Cycling was one of our shared hobbies and around this time we treated ourselves to a week's holiday with Duncan going to stay with my parents, which was a happy arrangement for all. Derek and I hired a motor-home and took our bikes up to the Lake District. It was while we were staying in a caravan park that the idea of running our own campsite occurred to us. From the outside I thought it looked like a doddle and would give us the outdoor life and independence we wanted. Derek agreed and we began to look for the ideal site. It was not at all easy. Either the site was beautiful but the house that went with it was disappointing, or we'd find a lovely house with a hopeless site.

We spent a year going out almost every weekend looking at sites to find the perfect one. Our criteria were a spacious site in a good location which was beautiful for visitors but also near a secondary school for Duncan, plus a nice house. Finally we found what we were looking for. A 16-acre site set in the most beautiful position high up on the Devonshire coast overlooking the sea outside the seaside town of Sidmouth. It took time for the purchase to be completed so we moved temporarily into a rented place in Wimborne, and for about six months Duncan went to the Queen Elizabeth School, the local comprehensive. Fortunately he was a very adaptable, sociable boy and easily gathered friends along the way. Both Derek and I were hugely excited about our new venture. My mother, in the typical way she had always joked about the various escapades in my life, just said: 'Poor man, he doesn't know what he's taking on.'

chapter nine

A New Start

When we hit on the idea of investing in a caravan park, one of the most appealing aspects was how easy it would be. Just a question of sitting back and taking the money as the bookings came in, I imagined. How wrong could I be? That first season Derek and I slaved non-stop from dawn to dusk and were so exhausted at the end of every day we could hardly speak. Yet despite the hard work we were also buoyed up by the excitement of realising our dream to own a beautiful place and create the lifestyle we wanted.

We moved in during the winter and as the days began to lengthen and the first spring flowers appeared, the beauty of the site and its location gave us such pleasure. Set high above the town of Sidmouth and just outside the village of Salcombe Regis the site covered 16 acres. It was a very tranquil, relaxing place to be with wide open spaces as well as lots of room between the pitches for the tents and caravans. All around us was farmland

and the view across the fields to the sea and the beaches of the Devonshire coastline was spectacular. Although Sidmouth was only five minutes away we felt we were in the heart of the country. I loved the house, too. It was designed to look like a barn from the outside, though it was a modern house. The big open-plan kitchen had an Aga and outside there was a courtyard with a duckpond and outbuildings.

However, to begin with we had only two members of staff: myself and Derek. Although it had been a very well-run site we wanted to make improvements and build it up, and that meant all the money had to be ploughed back into the business, leaving nothing for staff salaries. In high season I couldn't believe how much there was to do. We had to clean the toilet block three times a day and change-over day, Saturday, was frantic. All the caravans had to be cleaned, then I took the bed linen to the launderette in the wash block to put through the machines and iron. In between that someone had to be on duty in the site shop and Duncan's first Saturday job was helping me out there. He was brilliant with the customers and the natural charm he'd had as a little boy was very much in evidence. We also had to make time for all the visitors and business people who needed to speak to us. Our season started before Easter and in the height of summer, when we had a full complement of touring tents and caravans as well as all the static caravans, it was manic, simply full-on.

One of the most exciting and rewarding aspects of having our own business was being in control and thinking how to make improvements. Our year spent touring round looking at other sites had been valuable research. We extended the wash block and put in new showers and basins. In one or two areas the site seemed a little too open and Derek, who had invested in a tractor, planted more trees to improve the landscape. I felt little touches also mattered, like putting fresh flowers in all the caravans. The shop was another area ripe for improvement. Previously it hadn't carried a huge range but we went to the cash-and-carry and went mad stocking up on sweets and ice creams for the children and all the camping bits and pieces people needed, as well as lots of tinned goods. After a while we got a licence to sell alcohol so we could stock Devonshire cider and beer. I experimented with all kinds of things. One summer I did bacon sandwiches and another I found some sloe berries growing in the hedgerows and made sloe gin. I also sold fresh eggs once my hens were all laying well, because our love of animals meant we soon had quite a menagerie installed in the courtyard at the back of the house. It was a large area and we put netting up to keep foxes out, though the children staying on the site could come in to see the ducks and the 30 or so hens I had. Derek loved birds and he had a big aviary with parrots, which were something he'd always wanted to keep. At one time we had quails and sold quail's eggs.

The first year we were there Derek bought me a Yorkshire terrier as a present. He was the most adorable little scrap of fur with a big personality, and I called him Gordon. The following year we bought another, a bitch, as I wanted to breed. We called her Poppy and were very excited when she was expecting her first litter. Sadly though it was a rather heartbreaking experience. One puppy was stillborn and then Poppy herself got poorly and rejected the remaining two puppies. Duncan and I took turns getting up in the night to feed them with bottles but they were just too tiny and didn't pull through. I was terribly upset and so was Duncan, who is as soft-hearted as me about animals. The following year, however, Poppy had another litter of three puppies and this time she stayed healthy and was a brilliant mother. We kept them for a while and I would walk around the campsite with a little pack of five Yorkshire Terriers in tow.

We had brought Dakar with us and just before we'd moved had invested in another pedigree Main Coon, this time a female who we called Paris and hoped to breed from. Unfortunately she slipped out one night when she was in season and was pounced on by a rather ordinary tabby tom. The result was three adorable kittens, who we couldn't resist keeping. In total we ended up with 11 cats on the campsite.

We didn't stop at dogs, cats, hens, ducks, quails and parrots either. I had the sweetest little brown-and-white pygmy goat called Pandora who was exceptionally friendly and tame. She came for walks with me around the site, on a lead when the visitors were there and just following me loose when the site was empty. I even gave her piggy-backs. I got down on all fours and she climbed on my back and put her front hooves over my shoulders so I could carry her around. Later we got a second, black-and-white goat we called Billy.

Duncan was happy too. He settled easily into Sidmouth College, the local comprehensive school, and quickly made friends who often came to see him at the campsite, which was a pretty fun place for boys that age. They loved the animals and the wide open spaces were perfect for bike-riding. Unfortunately the school was too far away for him to ride to and there was no bus service, so every morning I drove him down the long hill into Sidmouth and collected him after school. As he headed into the teenage years it got harder and harder to get him out of bed on time and I would have to hammer on his door again and again. We were late practically every day.

Duncan had the biggest room in the house. It was long and set into the roof with Velux windows. When his friends came round they would all dive up there. I realised what my mother had gone through with my bedroom, as Duncan's room was always untidy with crisp packets, empty tins of soft drink and clothes all over the place. There was a big craze at the time for American wrestling and Duncan was completely into it. His room was full of posters, videos and books about American wrestling and he wanted to go and see live fights, which wasn't my kind of thing at all. Fortunately I had a very good friend called Pat whose son was also mad on it, and her parents very kindly took the two boys to all kinds of live shows around the South-West.

I had met Pat years earlier during one of our trips to the seaside at Bournemouth and her son Andrea was the same age as Duncan. She had a much younger son as well but, like me, was on her own. Her parents were very supportive in looking after her youngest child, so Pat and I did lots of things together with the boys. On one such occasion the four of us went to spend the day in Poole. The boys, who were 11 then, were absolutely mad on slot machines. We loaded them up with change and went to wait for them in a wine bar on Poole quay. We took it in turns to go back and check on them but they were set to be there for hours. We were so long in the wine bar we got chatting to other people there and some guys who had a speedboat moored on the quay invited us to go for a ride with them around the harbour. Poole Harbour is not just a tiny conventional harbour but a really huge natural harbour with Brownsea Island in the middle. By now we were pretty bored just waiting for the boys so we decided they'd never miss us for half an hour and got in the boat. In fact we were far longer than half an hour and when we got back, having stopped off in the boat at another bar on the way, we were horrified to see Pat's parents parked on the quayside with the boys sat in the back looking daggers at us. They'd come to find us and when they couldn't, Andrea had phoned his grandparents who'd promptly driven over from their home in Bournemouth.

Both our sons and Pat's parents were in the blackest of moods, but fortunately we were soon forgiven.

The American wrestling craze lasted for quite a while, after which Duncan's birthday presents reflected whatever the craze was at the time. We went through skateboards, Gameboys, a Nintendo games machine and special speakers. An especially prized present was a huge Yamaha keyboard, which replaced the small one he'd had for years, and Duncan spent ages messing around on that creating songs and writing lyrics. Different fashion statements accompanied these crazes. I particularly hated the baggy trousers with the crotch round the knees look. The teenage years can be a time when parents drift apart from their children, but we stayed close and I always felt I could say anything to Duncan, and he felt the same. When I said, 'Don't wear those trousers, you look awful in those,' he just said, 'Shut up mother,' but in such an affectionate way that it wasn't offensive at all.

Duncan wasn't a tough boy, rather he was very gentle and intuitive, and the sensitive side of his nature was always apparent. He started Sidmouth College in the third year, while all the rest had been there since the age of 11, which could have been quite a challenge but Duncan always made friends very easily. His only slight problem was that as a newcomer he attracted rather a lot of attention from the girls and that made the boys a bit jealous, but that soon settled down and he made lots of good friends among the boys too. Duncan's friends have always been very important to him. After moving to Sidmouth he stayed in touch with a boy called Paul from Blandford whom he'd known from when he was eight and who is still a good mate today.

Duncan's relationship with Derek was never close and there was no sense in which Derek became a father-figure to him. Instead my parents remained very central to Duncan's life. They both came down to stay with us but more often Duncan and I drove up to them, which took about an hour and a half, to have Sunday lunch. Duncan would often play the piano with my father. We both loved that. If it was high season and I couldn't get away I would leave Duncan to stay a night or so with them. All three of them derived great pleasure from those visits.

In his retirement from teaching my father filled his life with all kinds of voluntary work and causes, delivering Meals-on-Wheels and driving people without transport to hospital appointments. He was a man of huge energy and was always looking for ways to contribute to the community and also the church. My mother also filled her days very happily. Like me she was a great animal lover, and whenever possible she'd always owned a dog. Going out walking was one of her great enjoyments and when the black labrador she'd had for many years, Sita, sadly died, she contacted the local animal rescue centre. They had a young Belgian Shepherd bitch called Terri needing a home and my mother was particularly delighted because before Sita she'd had a German Shepherd, and only switched to labradors when Duncan was born because they were better with small children. By now my parents had moved from the house in Blandford, 'High Trees', where Duncan spent his early years, to a smaller place, but Duncan still had his own bedroom when he wanted to stay.

During the second season we saw an increase in our bookings and were able to take on staff. It was a relief to have a Saturday girl to help with the laundry and by the end we had a manager to oversee the site, but it took a long time and a lot of hard work to get to that stage. As success gradually took the pressure off Derek and me, leaving more time for us to enjoy the life we'd created, differences between us began to show. I was far more sociable than him and loved to have people coming and going all the time. Now we'd created the lifestyle, I wanted to live it. I loved people coming up and enjoyed cooking big meals. I wanted to share this lovely life with other people who could drop in and see the animals, have a coffee or a glass of wine. But Derek wasn't such a people-person. One of his hobbies was off-roading and when he was away for a weekend on a trip and the weather was lovely I sometimes used the opportunity to invite my girlfriends round. Duncan asked his friends too and it would often turn into a bit of a party.

Duncan's 16th birthday marked something of a new stage in his life. From being small for his age he suddenly shot up in height, (he's now 5ft 11in) and he also gained the key to a new independence in the form of a moped. Living where we did he'd been reliant on me for lifts everywhere but now he could get down the long hill from the campsite into Sidmouth, both for school and for going out with his friends. Duncan was thrilled, but of course, that moped was the only thing that really gave me cause to worry during his teenage years. I was so nervous he'd have an accident, and if he was late back I would lie awake listening and breathe a huge sigh of relief when I heard him arrive home safely. I hated that time, I was so frightened, especially in the winter when it was dark and the rain made the roads treacherous.

Apart from fears of him having an accident I was very lucky – Duncan was always so considerate all through his teenage years as he knew I would worry. He always phoned me to let me know where he was and what time he would be home. I never had to worry about him drinking and he didn't smoke cigarettes. I worked with Derek seven days a week on the campsite, and from that point when Duncan had his own transport he tended to do his own thing and spent most of his time in Sidmouth. I didn't know what he was up to because he never told me, but I knew it was a safe place and I trusted him. He had lots of friends and messed about, but I always knew he wouldn't do anything really bad. One friend, John Hurson, did have a bit of a reputation and one of the teachers at the school warned me he was a bad influence on Duncan. To me, though, John was always terribly polite and had very good manners. In some senses he took Duncan under his wing and both protected him and taught him a lot, but perhaps not always the things I wanted him to know.

Duncan was a bit of a flirt and there were plenty of girls around, but the one he had a huge crush on for about three years was a girl called Kelly Ford. Duncan's weakest subject was maths and he spent pretty much the whole time in those lessons passing notes to Kelly, who sat behind him in class. When Duncan moved into the sixth form he and John Hurson came in for a lot of attention from the first and second-year girls, who actually went as far as to form a fan club for the two of them. The girls constantly sent them love letters, presents and sweets and used to say they were going out 'Duncanising' and 'Hurson Hunting' to look for them. I only found out about it because things got to such a pitch that the two boys were called into the headmaster's office and accused of encouraging the girls. In fact they weren't at all, which the head accepted. Both boys of course had their attention set on rather older girls, but that did little to dispel the fantasies of the younger students.

Duncan would never have brought a girl back to stay the night – I would never have allowed it – but I did walk in on a rather intimate scene at a party Derek threw to celebrate my 40th birthday. We hired a wine bar in Sidmouth and had karaoke, during which Duncan and a pretty girl who was the daughter of a friend of mine both got monumentally drunk. I walked into the wine bar toilet and interrupted them at a critical moment which could have been embarrassing, except that the next morning they were so hungover they scarcely remembered.

To earn money Duncan took on lots of after-school and weekend jobs. His natural charm and ability to get on with everyone meant he was always a success when he had to deal with the public. Even when he didn't like the job much, he usually had a good relationship with his boss. In this way he was a big hit with the owners of a large Sidmouth Hotel, although the job he was doing as a porter wasn't really up his street. The job he did love was working as an usher at the Ragway Cinema, a lovely old-fashioned cinema in Sidmouth with stalls and a circle. He had ice creams set out in a tray and a torch in the traditional way. He retained that interest in people he'd had since he was a small boy and took a shine to the lady who sat in the ticket box, telling me: 'She's lovely, Mummy, really lovely.'

When it came to schoolwork, every parents' evening told the same story. I went by myself, as I had done all through his school days, and enjoyed hearing the teachers say what a lovely personality he had and how he was a joy to have in the classroom. Then would come the second part: he could try harder, he didn't always concentrate and needed to work more consistently. The truth was he was pretty lazy and far preferred to play than work. He was always doing his homework on the bedroom floor five minutes before he was supposed to be at school. He never worried that his teachers would be upset and though I nagged him to work harder it was water off a duck's back. Nevertheless he did reasonably well in his GCSEs and went on to do an A-level in Theatre Studies.

The spring he turned 18 we hired a village hall for a fancy-dress party. Duncan and his friend John Hurson both wore top hat and tails, and Derek and I bought him his first car, a Fiat Uno. It was generous of Derek because by now cracks had begun to show in our relationship. We had come so far with our dream lifestyle, but once we had acheived everything we'd worked for the differences between us were too great. Derek just wanted a quiet, peaceful life and to him I was like a whirlwind. I wanted people and happenings and I felt frustrated. My mother's words of warning came back to me. But crucially, one thing I will always be grateful to Derek for is the support he gave me early on in our relationship while I underwent what was to be one of the most emotional experiences of my life.

chapter ten

Roots

When I set up home with Derek, before we moved to Sidmouth and the campsite, I began to think more and more about my birth mother. Somehow living away from my parents made such thoughts possible. A change in the law had given adopted children the right to see their birth certificates and there began to be stories in newspapers and magazines of people who had tracked down one or both birth parents. I belonged to a generation of babies given up for adoption after the war. Many of us had become parents ourselves and were asking questions and feeling the need to know and understand our roots.

I had hesitated before mostly out of a sense of loyalty to my adoptive parents. I couldn't bear to hurt or upset them, but now mine and Duncan's lives were firmly independent I felt more confident that I could keep it a secret. I talked a lot to Derek about why I felt I wanted to do it – it was part of finding out and understanding who I was – and he was wonderfully supportive and encouraging. As a child it had never occurred to me that my mother even existed in the same timescale that I lived in. It had seemed that she must be almost from another age, another world. Now I began to realise she would quite likely be only in her fifties and exist as a real flesh-and-blood person. I burned to ask her so many questions to fill in the missing pieces of my story.

I thought I would have to go through agencies, which I was loathe to do – I didn't want strangers to ask me about something so deeply personal. I started off trying to contact St Catherine's House in London for information about my birth certificate but it meant a personal visit. So I decided to try a much more direct route. On a trip to my parents I revisited the black tin box that had held such fascination for me as a young teenager. The book of tokens for free milk was still there. I don't know why my parents kept it. They simply put everything in that box. Maybe they hung on to them either consciously or subconsciously because they contained a clue that I would eventually find. I'll never know, but I was grateful that they had. My mother's name had long ago burned itself into my mind and I scribbled down the simple address, consisting of just a street number, the name of a road and Leeds.

I sat down and wrote a letter to that address explaining that I wanted to contact a woman called Audrey McCormack, though I didn't give the reason. I included my telephone number as well as my address. I felt it was very unlikely that anyone at that address would still have any contact with or knowledge of the family. After all, this was more than three decades later and her parents, if that was their address, might be dead or have moved many times since. The most I felt I could hope for was a lead from whoever lived there now that would take me to another address.

Three days later I got a phone call. It was from a man called James who said he had received my letter and asked why I wanted to contact Audrey McCormack. I told him my story and he said Audrey was his sister. He was my uncle, born many years after her but only 11 years before me. None of his family lived at the address I had written to but neighbours had known how to contact him. He was the only member of the family still living in the Leeds area but obviously he had all his sister's details and said he would contact her. My legs felt wobbly and a heady mixture of excitement and anxiety swept over me. The shock of that immediate connection was intense. It surprised me how easy it had been to make the link with my roots after all those years entertaining the idea of a mythical mother who was remote and impossible to find or know.

Twenty minutes later the phone rang again and a woman's voice, sounding nervous, said, 'Fiona? This is Audrey.' I began crying, she did too. I wanted to know what had happened to her and she wanted to know about my life. It was like two halves of a jigsaw coming together. Neither of us knew the other one's story. She had been 21 and single when I was born. I was the result, she said, of a love affair that didn't last and she hadn't kept in touch with my father. She had since been married and had one son, Paul, but the marriage had ended. Subsequently she had met a chap who was younger than her and had gone to live in Spain, but that was in the past too. I told her I'd had a blissfully happy childhood and that my parents were very loving. She was so relieved and glad to hear that. I told her also how I'd fantasised about her and sometimes dreamed of having a young, glamorous mother.

I wanted to meet her and she agreed. She was living not far from Leeds and we fixed a date for the following week. Derek was going to drive me up and Audrey suggested a hotel near where she lived where we could stay and where she would get a taxi to meet us. I was glad she suggested that because I don't think I could have coped with going to see her at her home. We both somehow felt we needed to meet on some kind of neutral territory.

Derek and I drove up during the day. I told no one else what I was doing. I knew Duncan would feel very anxious because he had such an intense loyalty to his grandparents, and at his age would have found it hard to understand the burning desire I had to know who I was.

The hotel was modern and anonymous; the kind used by business people. Derek and I checked in and then it was a question of waiting. We had arranged to meet at seven in the evening, which was the time Audrey could most easily come along. We ordered some sandwiches in our room but I had no appetite. My stomach was churning and I couldn't concentrate on anything. When the phone finally rang I was so keyed up it made me jump.

'Audrey McCormack is in reception,' said a voice. It felt dream-like, unreal. I was about to meet a perfect stranger who, 34 years earlier, had held me as a tiny baby in her arms. We went down in the lift, the doors opened and there was one woman in her fifties standing alone in the lobby looking at me. I stepped forward and then we both spontaneously put our arms round each other and began hugging and hugging and almost immediately there were tears running down my face and a terrible lump in my throat. This was the woman I had been thinking about all my life, and here it was finally happening. It was like finding part of myself. I could feel her trembling, shaking and became aware she had tears on her face too.

Derek managed to shepherd us out of the lobby and into a secluded corner of the bar. When we sat down she just stared at me a lot. *Really* stared at me. She was clearly overwhelmed and found it hard to speak. I understood something of the mixed emotions she was experiencing. I had opened up her past, which she had struggled with and tried to bury for all those years. Now it was just there, sitting in front of her face, whether she wanted it to happen or not.

For my part I had never experienced an emotion like it in my life.

It was most peculiar. Here was a woman who was supposed to be my mother but I didn't know anything about her. I hadn't even seen a picture of her before, though thankfully I knew immediately I liked her. There were none of the feelings I had for my adopted mother, who had brought me up. No mother-daughter bond. How could there be? But there was a sense of familiarity and, even in my emotional state, I was instantly aware of similarities. She had the same colouring, height and build. Her clothes and manner struck a chord. Derek said it was like looking at two sisters.

Then she rummaged in her bag and pulled out a brown envelope. Inside was a little black-and-white snapshot of a baby. I knew it immediately. It was the same picture of me aged about three months that was in my parents' family albums. It was a strange moment.

The next day I went to her house, where she lived alone, and Audrey told me her story:

'We were a Catholic family and having a pregnant unmarried daughter was a terrible disgrace. My mother was half-Italian and my father came from Ireland. I was the second of four daughters and then we had a younger brother, James, born in 1942. The following year my father was killed in a motorbike accident and my mother was left on her own to bring us all up, which was very hard for her. She never remarried.

When I realised I was pregnant I told no one at first. I kept it hidden from my mother, which wasn't hard as I was slim and wore baggy clothes. It was my elder sister Maureen who guessed and told my mother, who was very upset and demanded to know who the father was. I wouldn't tell her, which made her even more furious.

At that time in my life I had a habit of falling madly in love with people and I had been in a relationship that I'd kept hidden from my mother because he wasn't Catholic, he was Jewish. We were together nearly a year. By the time I knew I was pregnant our romance had finished but I still cared about him and I wanted to protect him. Also I had read a story in the local paper that really frightened me. It involved a court case in which a non-Jewish girl with an illegitimate baby had said the father was a member of a well-to-do Jewish family. The family retaliated in court with terrible stories about the number of men they claimed she had slept with.

My sister Maureen, who was three years older than me, was married with a little girl and she was expecting a second baby soon after mine was due. I stayed living at home but it was Maureen who took over and looked after me. There was a Catholic home for unmarried mothers in the area called St Margaret's, and it was my sister who took me to make the arrangements to have the baby *there and for it to be adopted. No one ever suggested I could think of keeping my baby. In 1956 it was simply a terrible disgrace to be pregnant and single.*

I went into the home a few weeks before the baby was due. Once it got to this point my mother put her anger aside and became very supportive. She came to visit me as often as she could and used to bring me cigarettes, which might seem odd now, but in those days no one had any idea of the risk of smoking, especially when pregnant, and I was always puffing away.

There were several other girls in the home so we all did what we could to support each other and we had a great deal of hard physical work to keep us busy: scrubbing the floors, doing all the cleaning, washing and cooking. There was also a great deal of praying and the priest visited often. The nuns all had a 'holier than thou' attitude. They were very fond of the babies when they arrived but they thought we were disgraceful.

No one told us anything at all about the birth or looking after babies. They had a delivery room and there was a nurse, a big fat woman, who was quite nice. Every so often someone would go into labour and would be taken off into this room and we would all wonder what was happening. I was petrified. I've blocked out what happened during the birth because it was so bad. We had no painkillers. My baby weighed just over 7lb and I looked after her myself from the start and breastfed her, which is what we were all expected to do. At night they put the babies in a nursery and brought them to us when they woke and wanted feeding. I called my baby Paula because at the Kodak factory where I'd worked previously there'd been a model with that name and I was very struck by it. We had a christening and the priest, who was often around, came to the home.

Before she was born I'd signed an agreement saying I'd give her up for adoption, so there was never any question of anything different happening. I kept her for six weeks, which was the agreed time, and I always knew the date when I'd have to give her up. She was born on February 20th so it was the end of March when a couple came to collect her. I got her dressed and ready and one of the nuns took her from me. I never met the couple who took her or knew anything about them at all, but I did catch a glimpse of them. I wasn't supposed to, but I went into one of the rooms that looked out down the road and I saw their car driving off. All I could see was that the woman had red hair.

The next day I packed my own things, left the home and went back to live with my mother to try to get on with my life. For the first few weeks I couldn't do anything but cry. I was so upset. But I never discussed it with my mother. We never talked about what happened. It was a disgrace to the family. The rules at the home were that we were allowed one photograph of the baby to be sent to us from the adopted parents which was taken when she was about two or three months old but I never saw it because it was sent to my mother. She simply put it away in an envelope and never gave it to me. I suppose she thought it was best that I try to put the baby out of my mind.

Twenty years later when she died we were sorting out her things and among her documents was a small, brown, unmarked envelope. Inside was a photo of a little baby. I knew immediately who it was. That was the only picture I had.

I didn't go back to the Kodak factor after the baby was adopted. Instead I got a job on the buses in Leeds because the money was very good and I had to repay my mother for the time she'd supported me when I hadn't worked. We wore a uniform and inspectors used to check our badges were straight. I buried my baby very deep in my subconscious, although when I married and had my son four years later I called him Paul and it brought back a lot of feelings. I used to look for my little girl's face when I scanned the crowds on the streets of Leeds, focusing on *children who were the right age. I didn't know she'd gone from Leeds.*

I sent a letter to the home saying if anything happened to the couple who adopted her or if she tried to find me to get in touch, but I heard nothing. I had been wondering all my life what had happened to her. I felt such a sense of guilt for giving my baby away and I just hoped that the family were good and kind. That was the reason I went through with the adoption – to give my baby the chance of a better life than I could give her.

I didn't know new laws allowed people to trace their parents so as the years went by my hopes weren't high that I would ever see or hear of my only daughter again. At the time I had the baby my little brother James was only 11 and although he must have picked up something of what happened I never talked of it with him. It was buried too deep in my subconscious. When James called me he said, 'Did something bad happen to you when you were in your early twenties, because there's someone trying to contact you.'

I knew immediately it must be my daughter. I felt a great surge of emotion inside me and I longed to know what had happened to the baby I'd given away. I rang the number James gave me immediately. I had no idea what I would hear and it was such a relief to be told of a happy, loving childhood. Our meeting was a very emotional event for me. I didn't take anyone with me. Maureen now lives in Wales but I've always done everything alone – it's a matter of pride. It was a very hot evening and I was extremely nervous as well as excited. When I saw her I just burst into tears. We both did. She looks like my double, everybody says so. I couldn't get over the way she looked. Every feature of her face was like mine.

My first impressions were that she was confident and spoke very clearly. When I was younger I was very extrovert and we are so similar. It's not just our looks that are the same; we share so many of the same personality characteristics and tastes. I loved ballroom dancing and also amateur dramatics. There is a theatrical line in the family. My sister Maureen nearly took it up as a career; she used to be the producer and I acted in our local amateur dramatics. Fiona told me how she loved ballet and wanted to be a dancer. The genes were crying out for recognition. Since then I've often thought about the similarities in our lives – we even became single mothers at about the same age too. I wanted her to know every member of the family, to know her roots.'

*   *   *

Shortly after our first meeting I came up to stay with Audrey. I wanted to know all about her and her family, my family, and she wanted me to meet them too. Audrey asked me if I'd like to see the nursing home where I was born and I said yes. It was no longer run as a home for unmarried mothers but was still owned by the Catholic Church. I went inside and there was a very cold, clinical atmosphere which Audrey said was just the same as when she was there.

We drove past the house where she lived with her mother, who had since died, and then she took me round to meet everybody. She was very proud of me. Everyone was very interested and made a fuss of me, which was so kind of them. Though Audrey was stoic, I could see a terrible sadness in her face. I knew it was a big struggle for her and I knew she was doing this because she felt she owed it to me.

The first person I met was James, her younger brother, who had been the initial link. Although he was my uncle he was only 11 years older than me, and I took to him immediately. He was married with two sons and he and his wife were so welcoming and friendly. I was a bit embarrassed because he'd been a young boy when it all happened and didn't really know anything about me until out of the blue my letter was passed to him.

Next I met Maureen, Audrey's older sister, who had been a tower of strength to both Audrey and, I think, their mother throughout the pregnancy. She also immediately put me at my ease, welcoming me to their family. She is such a kind and sharing person and has a daughter, Cath, who is now a teacher and lives in Dartford. Then there was Christine, another of Audrey's sisters who was equally welcoming and who has a daughter, Amanda, now living in Birmingham. In one day I met two or three branches of this huge family and it was a very strange feeling. I was being told, 'This is your cousin', and 'This is your aunt or uncle', and it was bewildering. I couldn't immediately think of all these strangers as my relatives or understand what part they would play in my life.

Amid all those feelings, however, was a sense of peace at having found Audrey and discovered who she was. I felt very emotional towards her and told her I loved her. She said the same and wrote me some wonderful letters. Not long after we met something happened that crystallised some of those feelings. Her son Paul called to say that Audrey had had an accident and had broken her ankle and was in hospital. He thought I would want to know, which I of course did. I called the hospital to ask about her and they wanted to know who I was. I said, 'I'm her daughter.' It was the first time I'd made that statement. I wanted to say it and I felt proud to be able to. It was a good feeling and I could tell Audrey felt really happy to be able to use that phrase too, saying to people, 'my daughter's coming to see me.'

Audrey has so many characteristics similar to mine. In her youth she was quite extrovert and also had a more strongly artistic side. It was strange looking at her and seeing so much of myself.

Her little tops, long floral skirts, dangly earrings and varnished nails were just me. We'd even coloured our hair the same, with reddish tones. Inside her house, her mantelpiece could have been mine. Everywhere were animal ornaments of ducks and cats, little picture frames and soft furnishings. I was shocked, it was so uncanny. On her wall were paintings she'd done when she was younger – she was a talented artist – and they depicted all the things that I love, fields and poppies, scenes of nature. Her home furnishings were me too, the cushions and curtains could have been in my home. It was amazing that we had never had anything to do with each other yet we were so alike.

I've always been aware, in the way people are of imperfections they don't like, of a tiny red vein I've got just below my right nostril and I noticed, that first evening we met, that Audrey had an identical one in exactly the same place. There is such a strong genetic link between us, and yet her son Paul looks nothing like her at all. Audrey says he is exactly like his father while I've got all her genes. Before I met Audrey I was never able to say what my family medical history was. I had to shrug 'I don't know'. Fortunately there weren't any horrible health problems to be revealed. On my father's side I still don't know, and I am not sure if I will ever go so far as to try to seek him out. At the moment it's not important to me.

Audrey, in turn, wanted to know about my childhood and it made her feel good to hear I'd had such a happy, secure upbringing. She knew my adopted parents were an army couple and I told her they were very good people who had given me total love and affection. I also told her that I'd had moments of wishing I had a younger mother who was a little more unconventional and not quite so conservative. Once I'd met Audrey I imagined what my life would have been like if I hadn't been adopted. I would have loved having such a youthful, flamboyant mother, but I wonder though if I would have had the stability and security that I've had from my parents, because that is what every child needs. Audrey had quite a hard, tough life, moving around a lot, and I would have had to move around with her.

I still felt churned up after that second visit. It took a long time for all the emotions to settle down. There was the question, after my curiosity was satisfied, of what part we would play in each other's lives now and in the future. I knew I wanted her in my life. I didn't want to contact her just to discover my roots and then not have any more to do with her. There was the problem, however, of keeping her hidden from what I felt was my true family because I didn't want to cause them hurt in any way. This included my brothers as well as my parents. Audrey understood this but I decided to be honest with Duncan and tell him about her because it was part of his history as well as mine.

It was very hard for him as a teenager to understand why I had wanted to find her and that it didn't mean I loved my adopted parents any less. To me they were still my parents and always would be. Audrey came to stay with us at the caravan park a couple of times but at that stage Duncan kept her rather at arm's length and his attitude to me was, 'I hope you're not going to see too much of her.' It was hard to deal with because in every other way Duncan and I were so close, but I did understand. I kept her away from him during her visits and only phoned Audrey when he wasn't around. It was very sad that for years I could never talk about being adopted and now I couldn't talk about finding my real mother and all these new relatives.

There are no rules and some of my feelings were quite conflicting. After the initial euphoria I later went through a phase of feeling that Audrey had no right to call me her daughter. I didn't want her to assume I was *her* child because she gave her child away. On her side there was probably disappointment in me that I didn't play a bigger part in her life once we had met, or that Duncan didn't immediately form a relationship with her.

I went through many different types of emotion before Audrey and all my relatives could settle into a natural place in my personal landscape, and I think Duncan had to go through a similar, though less intense, process. More people have spoken now about finding their real parents, but in many ways that's the beginning of the story and what happens afterwards is an unknown quantity. People contemplating meeting their birth parents should be aware that the aftermath is not easy. You go through this ridiculous 'found them, got another family, stay in my life' stage but it's not that straightforward. There are big issues of guilt that I had to deal and live with.

Now Audrey is firmly in place in my thoughts. Settled. It's funny how that happens almost imperceptibly. You go through all that conflicting emotion and when you get through the other side you can put things in their place. The same is true for Duncan. Where first he was anxious and felt a fierce loyalty to his grandma and granddad and expressed that by keeping Audrey at arm's length, now he is very caring and accepts her place in his life.

The one thing I do feel very sad about that I can't change is that I didn't tell my parents. I think Duncan told my mother, although it never came to light and she never said anything to me. Duncan told me after she died that she knew because she had seen a card once from Audrey. I think Duncan perhaps helped her along the way and now he tells me she was waiting for me to go to her and tell her. The fact that I never did is another area of guilt I have to live with. But even though these things are hard I am a more complete person for having discovered my roots and I don't regret taking that step.

chapter eleven

Separate Ways

The cracks began to appear in my relationship with Derek several years before we finally split but I did my best to ignore them. Everything else was so perfect and we had managed, after years of hard work, to create the lifestyle we had both dreamed about and which had brought us together in the first place. But it became obvious that we were beginning to spoil that dream for each other. When I filled up the place with friends I could see irritation written all over Derek's face. I was walking on eggshells, always expecting him to take offence or show his displeasure by becoming moody or withdrawing in a huff. For my part I was confrontational and it led to some bitter rows between us.

After one spectacular late-night bust-up I felt I had to get away and put some space between us. I threw some things in the first bag to hand and, in a highly emotional state, drove off to Sidmouth with Duncan, who was then 15. I had no clear idea of what I was going to do except that I had to get away from the campsite. I parked in the town car park and when Duncan asked what we were going to do, I decided: 'We're going to stay in a bed and breakfast.' Of course being a seaside town there were hundreds of them to choose from. I got some money from the cash dispenser and knocked on the door of the first place I saw with a B&B sign. A man answered the door and claimed he had no vacancies. I couldn't tell whether it was because a distraught-looking woman and a teenage boy with scarcely any luggage arriving late in the evening fazed him, or whether they really had guests.

We walked on down the street and at random I picked another. This time a woman answered and said she had a room. As we went in, a fair-haired man appeared and took my bag, which I realised to my embarrassment looked more like something you'd take to the beach than an overnight bag. He was very charming, suppressing any curiosity he may have felt about the reason behind our visit and making us feel very welcome.

The next morning when we woke I felt so much better for having stayed away from the campsite. Duncan and I went down to breakfast. We were the only guests, and the charming, fair-haired man came to serve us. He was just as attentive, and now I could detect a trace of a Canadian accent. We got talking and Duncan, always friendly and open, told him that he was going to a rehearsal for a theatre production in which he had a key part. The Sidmouth theatre group he belonged to were staging an open-air performance of *A Midsummer Night's Dream* and had invited him to audition for the role of Puck. At that stage he still looked very young and was perfect for the role. When he won the part I was terribly proud. Duncan was thrilled because it was such a major role, requiring him to be on stage for much of the play. As Duncan relayed all this I could see our host was charmed by his manners and openness.

When Duncan and I returned to the campsite I felt guilty as I saw Derek's worried face. In our hearts we probably both knew our relationship wasn't going to last but we called an uneasy truce. Derek had never been very close to Duncan but he came with me to the performance of *A Midsummer Night's Dream*. More importantly for Duncan his beloved Grandma and Grandpa came down from Blandford and stayed in a local hotel on the night of the show. The setting for the performance – the floral gardens in the area of the town known as Jacob's Ladder – was magical. It was a modern interpretation of the classic play and Duncan's role as Puck was pivotal. He was the youngest member of the cast by far, as many of the other roles were taken by adult members of the drama group, and his was an impressive performance. They performed for a week and I was so proud when the local paper ran a flattering review.

Shortly after that I had reason to go to the doctor and she recognised my surname, asking me if I was anything to do with Duncan Inglis. When I said Duncan was my son she went into absolute raptures about the show and his performance, saying, 'My darling, darling Puck – he was so lovely.' It was the first recognition of Duncan's ability. He hadn't done much acting before but I'd always known he would end up finding success in some kind of performing. He had that kind of aura about him.

Theatre and acting became very important to Duncan. Every year when a troop of repertory players came down for the summer season at the local theatre he made friends with them. During the sixth form at Sidmouth College he did Theatre Studies with a drama teacher called Miss Davis. She was a charismatic and imposing woman, and the younger pupils were a bit frightened of her. Duncan was certainly in awe of her to begin with, but as he got older he found her inspirational. She was very good with teenagers and the sixth form were her special 'gang'. Under her direction they staged Leslie Bricusse's *Sherlock Holmes: The Musical* and Duncan was given the part of Dr Watson. He had to dress up as an old man and when I went to see the show I found the resemblance to my father remarkable. He was an excellent actor and I could tell immediately that he was imitating Grandpa. All the movements, the mannerisms and even aspects of speech were there, although of course only I could recognise them. It made for a really convincing performance. I have a copy of the picture that the local paper ran framed in my sitting room today.

But it was his singing ability that really surprised me. I didn't even know that up until that point that Duncan could sing so well. When he was small he was a very happy boy who was always singing in the bath and round the house, and I also knew he had a very good ear and could reproduce a tune. But hearing him in that musical was the first time I realised he had a real talent. I had been in the school choir and enjoyed singing but I certainly couldn't sing solo the way I discovered Duncan could. I talked to Miss Davis and she was equally encouraging and said she was pleased with his progress.

It was during Duncan's last year at school when, frankly, I didn't see much of him because he was always down in the town with his friends, that I began to brood more on what was wrong between Derek and me. As Derek didn't like going out much and I didn't want to sit alone with him up at the campsite, I got into the habit of going for a glass of wine or a coffee with girlfriends. Nine times out of ten I'm afraid I ended up boring them silly with my problems. One evening when we were in a wine bar in Sidmouth, a chap who looked vaguely familiar came over and asked, 'Do you remember me? You and your son, who was going to be in *A Midsummer Night's Dream*, came and stayed at my guesthouse.'

He offered to buy us all a drink and I became aware that he'd had a couple himself. He told me that he was born in South Africa but grew up mainly in Canada, and that the woman who had opened the door to me was his wife who was Canadian. He said there had been problems in the relationship and that since I'd stayed at their bed and breakfast his marriage had broken down and his wife had left him, returning to her relatives in Canada. I said nothing to him of my own marriage problems at that stage. He was simply a charming man with a quiet, sensitive manner who was lonely and glad to find a sympathetic ear to pour out his troubles to. At the end of the evening we said goodbye and I thought no more about it.

Some weeks later Duncan, who had a Saturday job working on the checkout at Summerfield's supermarket, said, 'That guy Tony from the bed and breakfast came through my till today and he asked after you.' Over the next few months Duncan seemed to come across Tony more and more frequently around Sidmouth. One day Duncan mentioned him again and gave a secret smile when he said his name. I asked him what the big joke was and he started laughing and said, 'Tony promised he'd buy me a drink if I could get you to go out with him.' I thought it was cheeky, even outrageous, because Tony didn't know anything about my situation, but it made me laugh to think he was bribing my teenage son in an attempt to meet me again.

Some time after that I came face to face with Tony by chance in Sidmouth. I didn't let him know that Duncan had spilled the beans about his attempt to see me again but I stopped for chat. This time, without a few drinks inside him, I discovered he could be entertaining and funny as well as soulful and sensitive. The tension in my relationship with Derek was making me feel increasingly lonely and the next time I had a bust up with him, instead of turning to my girlfriends, who must have been heartily sick of listening to my problems, I thought of talking to Tony. I walked around the town for a bit and then turned down the road where he lived. There was a 'for sale' sign up outside the bed and breakfast. I knocked and when Tony opened the door and saw me, his face lit up in a smile. 'I've just got to talk to someone,' I told him. Without asking any more questions he led me through to the kitchen at the back of house and made me a cup of tea. Knowing he'd had his own marriage difficulties made it easier to talk and he was a very good listener. It helped as well that he didn't know Derek, and that he saw things from a man's perspective and often challenged what I was saying.

After that I began to take myself off to his place for a tea and therapy session quite frequently. Instead of knocking at the front door I would walk down the path at the side to the back door and he'd make me a cup of tea and let me sit in his kitchen and rant about Derek. One afternoon I said I had to go early because I needed to walk my two Yorkshire Terriers, and Tony wanted to come too. From calling in now and again I began to visit regularly and we often took the dogs out for walks together.

Perhaps Duncan was aware of the subtle shift in my feelings for Tony even before I was, because one day, after he had met Tony and I walking the dogs, he teased me, saying, 'Don't let Derek find out.' He wasn't censorious because while Duncan had never been close to Derek, he felt something of a rapport with Tony. In fact I didn't hide my meetings with Tony from Derek. Tony was simply a friend with whom I went to have a cup of tea and a chat and I told Derek, quite honestly, that since we didn't get on I needed someone to talk to. He was cross and upset about my visits but I assured him, truthfully at that stage, there was nothing in it.

Then one day, when I was sitting in Tony's kitchen, the front doorbell rang. Tony answered it and there was Derek standing on the doorstep. He simply looked Tony up and down and said, 'So you're the guy that Fiona's coming round to have cups of tea with.' There was a bit of a pause and I wasn't sure what was going to happen but all Derek said, quite calmly, was, 'I just wanted to see what you look like.'

It was after that episode that I realised Tony really meant something to me. For ages I agonised about what to do, dreading scenes with Derek and the terrible upheaval, both emotional and practical, if we split. But Derek and I were driving each other nuts and one day, after I had arrived at Tony's house in tears, he kissed me and told me he loved me. He urged me to leave Derek and move in with him.

Tony was very much the opposite of Derek. Where Derek was practical, Tony was romantic, and where Derek found it hard to reach out to people, Tony had a natural empathy and intuition. I realised, once I had someone to talk to, that many of the sad feelings that had unexpectedly assailed me during the last couple of years were born out of a sense of loneliness. Once I understood that, I suddenly stopped feeling so cross with Derek, which was a

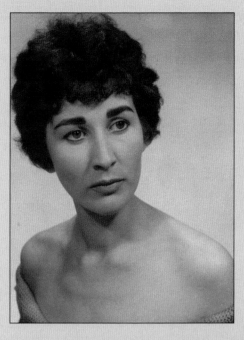

My birth mother
Audrey in her early
twenties. She always
modelled herself
on Audrey Hepburn's
glamourous look.

Audrey loved spending
time out of doors and
being close to nature.

With Audrey and my half-brother Paul on our first
meeting together.

Just the two of us, plus the family dog!

Duncan aged four. He was playing in his favourite mini-car in this snap taken by Alastair, who is a keen photographer.

Duncan chatting to 'his friend' on the beach at Bournemouth.

The clues added up to a masterpiece of youth

The Revenge of Sherlock Holmes, by Sidmouth Youth Theatre, reviewed by Mary Sinclair

NOW in it's eleventh year, Sidmouth Youth Theatre under the direction of Angela Davies has earned such high regard that it becomes a foregone conclusion that each new production will be superbly staged and performed.

The Revenge of Sherlock Holmes at the Manor Pavilion more than lived up to expectation. The Youth Theatre was privileged to present the amateur premier of the show which, written and composed by Leslie Bricusse, tells a lively tale of what really occurred following the death defying leap of the greatest detective in the world and his arch enemy Moriarty at Reichenbach Falls in 1897.

Our hero survives, but is listless and depressed now that there is no Moriarty against whom to pit his razor sharp wits. But then strange clues begin to emerge....Who is beautiful artist Bella Spellgrove? and how can Homes escape from Lestrade and an accusation of murder?

Swift

An excellently designed and constructed multiple set was the background for a swift succession of scenes and location. Liberally laced with lively chorus numbers and solo ballads, splendidly choreographed, and performed with expertise and panache by the 50-strong cast and 13 musicians under the baton of musical director Robert Millington, this production provided a feast of colour, sound and atmosphere, with some literally explosive effects.

There were some very able and mature characterisations from the young performers. In the title role, Jonathon Lister played with the strength and power we have come to recognise from him, managing the long complex phrases and speeches with understanding.

We all know that Holmes was a master of disguise, and Jon showed this aspect of the character to great effect with some amazing transformations; indeed, each time a new character appeared we began to suspect that it must be Homes yet again, and it usually was.

The fast and furious comedy number 'Apples and Pears', along with the cheery chorus, was one of the highlights of his performance.

As his trusty friend and assistant Dr Watson, Duncan Inglis gave a beautifully authentic performance, about as crystal clear and well judged a portrayal as it is possible for a teenage actor to achieve; gentle, convincing and never for an instant over the top.

Leading lady Nicola Berryman played the scheming beauty, Bella Spellgrove, with poise, grace and intelligence, and her singing - appearing effortless - was a delight. These three young principals carried their responsibilities commendably, and were well supported by Neil Kay as Inspector Lestrade, Mandy Patch as housekeeper Mrs Hudson, Angela Fulcher as the vengeful Mrs Moriarty, Michael Knight as Dr Boffy Martingdale, and Chris Day as Wiggins.

Other valuable contributions came from Richard Graham (Sir Jevons Jarndyce) Sarah White (Duchess of Monmouth) Greg Ward (PC Tomkins) Helen Hodge (Newsgirl) and Amy Wilson (the dying Maria).

Pace, tempo, interest and excitement all added up to yet another feather in the SYT's cap and show just what can be done when a skilled and dedicated teacher and director inspires an eager group of young people.

● WATSON ponders as the Youth Theatre triumphs again. Duncan Inglis played the good doctor.
Picture by Stuart Morton, ref. 2339:6.

Duncan as Doctor Watson in 'The Revenge of Sherlock Holmes' by the Sidmouth Youth Theatre. His review in the local newspaper reads, 'a beautifully authentic performance, about as crystal clear and well judged a portrayal as it is possible for a teenage actor to achieve.'

Another cutting showing Duncan as Puck in 'A Midsummer Night's Dream'.

Energy
The elfin-featured Duncan Inglis plays Puck with irrepressible exuberance, darting swiftly among the shadows bringing energy and vitality to the role and delivering his dialogue with an earnest anxiety that belies his tendency to anarchic mischief making.

Duncan with April (centre) and Rita (right) during their days as pop-band Tantrum.

One of my own photographic efforts! Duncan chilling out at home in 2001.

Duncan with his half-brother, Julian, and half-sister, Tara.

Duncan and I arriving at Liza Minelli's party to celebrate her husband's 50th birthday, May 2003.

At my first photoshoot with Duncan.

huge relief. Taking a step back I saw that our rows were not bitter personal attacks on each other. I realised that I had been asking him to be something he couldn't be.

Unfortunately, that realisation didn't make it any easier for me to talk to Derek and for a while I was pretty cowardly. By now Tony and I were totally smitten with each other. My love had taken a long time growing but then it really blossomed and I felt lucky to have met such a wonderful person. Tony, for his part, didn't care where we went or what we did as long as we were together. He was completely infatuated. He had been offered a good price for his guesthouse and the sale was going through. We talked of making a new start, away from Sidmouth. Tony wanted to buy another guesthouse and I suggested Bournemouth as a location. Together we began to plot and plan a life we could share.

By this time Duncan had left school and taken his first job as a rep with the local Haven Holiday camp just outside Sidmouth. He had wanted to go to drama school, but I couldn't afford to send him. The fees were phenomenally expensive and on top of that he would have had to pay for his own accommodation in London, so it was just not possible. Duncan was very resourceful though, and when that path was blocked he looked for other opportunities. He knew he wanted to do something that involved entertaining people and he loved singing and the theatre. When he saw the job advertised at Haven Holiday Camps he thought it would cover all those areas.

Once my affair with Tony became serious I wanted Duncan to be the first to know. I went to see him at Haven and told him I was going to leave Derek and that Tony and I planned to move to Bournemouth. Duncan liked Tony and he was pleased I'd found someone who made me so happy, but he was also worried about how Derek would react. I assured him it would be all right and that Derek and I were sorting it out, but secretly I was very anxious too.

In the event it was just about as awful as it could be. Despite all the problems we'd had, Derek was still very upset. I felt terrible, but all I could do was wish him well and tell him I was sorry it hadn't worked out. Tony and I had taken a six-month let on a rented cottage while we started looking for somewhere to buy. But a couple of days after I'd moved out Derek rang and said he wanted to talk to me. I went up to the campsite and he seemed much calmer and more focused.

'As well as a relationship we had a business together,' he said. 'A business we built up together and were proud of. There's still a good few weeks of the season left and you can't just walk out on the business side. I need your help to manage the site until it shuts down for the winter and I think you owe me that.'

I was taken aback but of course he was absolutely right. Now we had made the break all my dissatisfaction and anger had completely evaporated and I could see he was just taking a practical view.

'What are you suggesting?' I asked.

'The campsite doesn't close until the end of October. Will you come up for the remaining weeks and work for me? I'll pay you a wage and you can just come up here each day.'

So I agreed. Those were two of the strangest months of my life. I lived with Tony in Sidmouth but every day I drove up to the campsite and worked alongside Derek. The ironic thing is that during that time we became such good friends and got on better than we ever had before. To begin with we were slightly distant with one another. But gradually we began to talk. At first it was just about the business and how the day had gone. Then, over shared coffee breaks or sandwich lunches in the kitchen, we began to talk about our life together and where our relationship had gone wrong. Once we started we couldn't stop. Now that all the fighting had ended and the anger had disappeared, we were both able to open up with an honesty we had rarely achieved before. It didn't make either of us change our minds about parting but it felt good, for both of us, to be able to part with so much more understanding and affection in place of hostility.

'You've really thought about what you're giving up?' Derek asked me towards the end of the time. I said that I had, although inside I was also sad to say goodbye to everything we had worked for. My last day at the campsite was very difficult. I had so many belongings that I had to book a small removal van to collect them. Tony came up to help. Loading everything from my past life into the van and saying goodbye to Derek, who was very adult about everything but visibly sad, was horrible.

From the outset Tony warned me I would be going, as he put it, 'down the ladder' in terms of my standard of living if I chose to go with him. He'd seen the lovely house at the campsite and the comfortable lifestyle Derek and I enjoyed. He was worried about the fact that he couldn't provide the same and felt he had to tell me. For my part, I was completely infatuated with him and the practical aspects of our new life together seemed irrelevant. I only wanted to be with him and nothing else mattered.

Tony was always very sensitive to how I was feeling so when, one day, I took a call on my mobile phone and he saw me stop still in shock he was immediately concerned. The voice on the other end was one that I had buried, along with a lot of misery, nearly twenty years before.

'Hi Fiona, it's Simon here. Simon Roscoe.' I was quite unprepared for the immediate sense of flashback that I felt when I heard him again. For so many years, when Duncan was a baby and then a toddler, I had fantasised that Simon would call me and put everything right somehow. What epic words do you find to say to a man who has tried his hardest to utterly mess up your life and then calls like an old friend nearly two decades later? 'How did you get my number?' was the best I could manage. The answer was pretty simple. My parents were still living in Blandford, listed in the phone book, and Simon had rung claiming to be an old friend without revealing his true identity. My father, in all innocence, had handed over my mobile number.

There followed a slightly rambling tale from Simon, who said he had recently come back to Britain and had been sorting out some papers at his parents' house. He had come across an unopened letter I had written to him after Duncan's birth but before the terrible court case when he contested paternity. In the letter I had told him he had a son and how much I still loved him and that I hoped one day he would know that child and be proud. Evidently, the contents had moved him sufficiently to make the phone call. He wanted to tell me that his mother had never passed the letter on and that now, so long after I wrote it, he had finally read it for the first time. I didn't know whether to believe that, but when he said we should meet I agreed to take his number and think about it. Foremost in my mind was Duncan. He had never shown the slightest interest in knowing anything about Simon but I was aware that might change in the future. For myself there was a strong sense of unfinished business. I confided in Tony and although he was dubious about whether someone who had behaved so badly in the past could ever be a force for good in my life, he agreed that it would be prudent to know something about Simon in case Duncan expressed an interest further down the line.

For the moment I filed the number away. Tony and I were busy searching for the right business to buy. I had some money to invest in a partnership with Tony and we spent our days looking at all kinds of guesthouses along the south coast. We needed a business that would operate all year round, rather than a seasonal holiday bed and breakfast. Tony chose a guesthouse that was established as a commercial enterprise catering for business people of all kinds, from drivers to sales reps to people attending conferences and courses. It had eleven rooms to rent out and was situated on the main road into Bournemouth, so it was also well placed to attract casual trade. Duncan came over to see it soon after we moved in and I could see he was anxious about how I would adapt. He knew how much I loved the countryside and although I'd brought my two Yorkshire terriers with me, Gordon and Poppy, naturally I'd had to leave all my other pets behind with Derek. However, he liked Tony and he could also see that we were very much in love.

Tony was, quite simply, the most romantic man I have ever known. When we were sitting watching television he would suddenly pass me a little folded up note. Inside it would say something like: 'You look so lovely.' He was always finding thoughtful ways to surprise and delight me with small romantic gestures and tokens. Sometimes he would put a little bunch of fresh flowers by my bed or buy an unexpected present for no reason at all other than to show his love and affection. He wouldn't hear of me getting up early to make the breakfast for our guests. Of course if we were full and it needed two of us I did help, but otherwise Tony would get up very quietly and leave me sleeping.

When he'd served all the guests he would come back upstairs with breakfast on a tray for me.

My naivety about running a guesthouse was pretty well on a par with my initial ignorance about managing a campsite. I assumed sales reps and other business people would be invisible and silent in their rooms in the evening, appear to have breakfast, pay the bill and leave early. It's true we did have quite a few of those, but I soon discovered that other, very different types of people booked into guesthouses. Tony was not only kind hearted, he was also extremely tolerant and laid-back and at first he pretty well opened our house to anyone who knocked on the door. Not surprisingly that policy led to a few strange experiences.

One woman who had rented a room, I'll call her Jane, was so charmed by both Tony and the house that she didn't want to leave. Aged about 35, she said she had come down from Leicestershire and asked to stay for a week. During this time it became apparent to both of us that she suffered from some sort of mental illness, possibly schizophrenia. Her stay eventually extended over two months and she wanted to sign on as a permanent guest with the DHSS paying her rent. It was tragic because she was clearly fantasising about a place where she would feel part of a family. Although I'm not sure that her fantasies included me, as she became more and more demanding, wanting to see and speak to Tony at every opportunity. I suspect she must have stopped taking her medication because gradually episodes of odd behaviour began to impinge on other guests. We had a little bar where Tony would serve bar snacks and drinks in the evening. One night Jane's strange behaviour culminated in her threatening another guest at the bar. We realised she was unwell and helped get her to a doctor, but we couldn't cope with her living permanently with us, it was too much responsibility.

Then there was the terrifying morning when we woke to hear someone hammering on the front door at 5am. Looking out of the window as Tony threw on some clothes and ran downstairs, I saw a whole team of police with cars with flashing lights surrounding the front of our house. It turned out that a woman had gone to the police and accused one of our guests of raping her the previous evening. The police swarmed up the stairs and arrested their suspect, marching him from the house with his arms held behind his back, and proceeded to rip apart the room where he had been staying in a search for anything he might have hidden that would provide evidence. In the event he was cleared of all charges and the police concluded that the woman in question had made up the allegation, but it was a pretty shocking start to the day for us and, of course, a totally horrific one for him.

Another guest Tony accepted arrived on the doorstep in a terrible state with cuts and bruises and blood all over his shirt. He said he had been in a car crash but refused all our offers to get medical help. I was very worried and when I realised that he was an alcoholic, after his request the next morning to buy him a bottle of whisky, I was even more concerned. Fortunately when we weren't forthcoming with the booze he checked out after two days.

Even some of the guests who were apparently well off could present problems. One such visitor was a good-looking young Arab boy in his early twenties who had been recommended to us and wanted to stay several weeks while he attended a language course. His wealthy parents in the Middle East were funding his trip but after a while his overseas cash flow appeared to dry up and he stopped paying us rent. Asking always to speak to 'Mr Tony', our young guest kept assuring us his parents were going to pay. After many elaborate faxes back and forth to his parents in Dubai our guest left early one morning owing us three weeks' money.

Not surprisingly I found many of these escapades highly stressful and Tony's easy-going policy of open house to all-comers led to arguments between us. Tony was such a lovely man and got on with everyone, but he didn't discriminate between the commercial trade we wanted and the oddballs and crooks who knocked at our door looking for a temporary port in the midst of some kind of personal storm.

By this time, 1998, Duncan had left Sidmouth and moved to a Haven Holiday camp on the Isle of Wight. We spoke nearly every day on the phone and he came over to stay whenever he had a couple of days off. On one of these visits he brought me a cassette tape that was to change everything.

chapter twelve
Face to Face

Duncan was thoroughly enjoying working as a holiday camp rep. Like everything in his life, he pitched in and got the best out of what was on offer. After Sidmouth he worked at the Haven camp on Hayling Island and then moved to the Isle of Wight, a place he had visited with me on many of his childhood holidays. The job was part PR, at which he was a natural because of his excellent manner and his genuine interest in people, and part entertainer. He had to run bingo clubs and stage tea dances for the elderly, acting as the compere and taking a turn on the floor with some of the old ladies to get everyone up dancing. At the other end of the age spectrum he had to run children's clubs and also got the opportunity to take part in the stage shows laid on in the evening, singing all kinds of different material.

Even though he'd left home, Duncan and I stayed very close. Once or twice I went across to see him on the Isle of Wight, either taking a girlfriend or going on my own as Tony couldn't leave the guesthouse. Duncan always knew what was going on in my life. Often it was like talking with a friend, though my role switched depending on what was happening in his life. Sometimes I was very firmly in the maternal role, especially at times when he was struggling with a situation and asked for my advice. Like all mothers, I tried to give him the best advice I could, offering him encouragement and telling him to hang on in there if things were difficult. Most often the problems he faced were because he was absolutely hopeless with money. He was always extravagant and got into some terrible financial messes, piling up debts on credit cards and store cards. Not that any of it worried him unduly – Duncan was enjoying life to the full and always had a great capacity for living in the moment.

One day when he came over to stay for a couple of days with us at the guesthouse he brought a tape with him. He had been doing some singing at the camp, as well as messing around in his time off practising songs and trying out lyrics. He said he wanted me to listen to something he'd recorded with the help of the Entertainment Manager, who had played the piano while Duncan sang. When the tape began to play I was absolutely amazed. I heard a fantastic, deep voice that sounded so beautiful. I could not believe it was Duncan I was listening to! He was only 18 and had never had a singing lesson in his life, yet he had the voice of a professional. He sang a Michael Ball song, 'Love Changes Everything', and it reminded me of Michael Ball but I thought

Duncan's voice sounded even better. He also did an Elvis Presley number.

It has always been very important for Duncan to have my approval and when the tape finished he said: 'What do you think… do you really like it… are you sure?' I've always been totally honest with my son, even if sometimes he hasn't liked what I've said, but now I was in no doubt. It was absolutely brilliant and I told him so.

'You have got real talent,' I said. 'You must go to London and make a career out of that terrific singing voice.' We talked and talked about the best way to do it and Duncan said he had friends in London who would let him sleep on their sofa or doss down on the floor. I told him that each week he needed to get *The Stage*, the entertainment world's newspaper, and look for auditions to go to. I was convinced that with a voice like that he would be able to get work. Coupled with his acting ability, I imagined he stood a good chance of landing a part in the chorus of a West End musical. He handed in his notice at Haven and a couple of weeks later moved up to London. He was somewhat anxious but I've always given him loads of confidence and I just knew, one way or another, he would be successful.

Of course I wished I could have helped him out financially but what money I had was tied up in the guesthouse. Fortunately Duncan was always good at finding work and within a few days he rang to say he had a job as a waiter in an American fast-food restaurant. He enjoyed the work and was very good at it. Naturally the pay was pretty minimal but he got good tips. He got *The Stage* every week and began to apply for anything that seemed remotely possible.

Whenever I could I went with him to auditions. Often the adverts simply asked people to send in demonstration tapes of their singing so I helped him finance a demo tape which was recorded at a studio in Ringwood, Dorset. As Duncan was working during the day I often made the phone call to follow up when he'd applied for a show or a band. When I made the very first call, the girl I spoke to remembered his name and said, 'Oh yes, we heard the tape, he has such a nice voice.' Duncan was invited to come along and sing and we went up to a London theatre where the auditions were being held. I sat in the stalls when he was called up on stage. Although Duncan was very nervous I was convinced he was going to get the part because from the comments I heard I could tell everyone was impressed with him. When he got a letter a few days later saying he hadn't got it, I was really surprised and told him so. Duncan, however, was quite philosophical about it all. 'Oh well, let's try the next one,' he said, and he was quite prepared to give it as long as it took to get a break. At this stage he still hadn't had so much as a single singing lesson, but I didn't doubt his talent.

With Duncan and his career at the forefront of my mind my thoughts also turned to the question of Simon Roscoe. Everyone who has brought up a child as a single parent knows all too well those times when you want to share something, whether it's joy or anxiety, with the one other person who should care as much as you do. I had written Simon out of our lives and out of my mind all the time Duncan was growing up, but now I was so proud to see the man my son was turning into that I felt sure Simon would also be curious to know what Duncan was like. More than anything, since tracing my real mother I had become far more aware of the long-term importance for people, often later in life, of knowing their background. There was no indication that Duncan would ever want to go down that route but I felt I owed it to him to keep some lines of communication open.

Then there was the physical resemblance. Duncan was still several years younger than Simon had been when we'd met, but the likeness was already unmistakable. I felt Simon's phone call must mean he was curious about his son and I was pleased. I wanted to show him photographs and tell him all about Duncan's singing ability and let him in on what our son was trying so hard to achieve.

I also wanted to satisfy my own curiosity. This had been the all-consuming love affair of my most impressionable years and I wanted not just to know what had happened to the man who had broken my heart, but also to discover what I felt after all these years. Simon was living in Lulworth, not far down the Dorset coast from Swanage where we had spent our first weeks together. I called the number he had given me and said I had decided we should meet up. He sounded pleased and gave me the name of a little country pub on the road to Lulworth. Although Tony had been there when Simon made that initial call, I didn't tell him about the planned meeting as I knew he would immediately worry on my behalf. Besides, I felt I wanted to talk with Simon on my own to gauge his true feelings about Duncan and also to test myself. What would I feel when we met? It had to be a private meeting. In the event my visit to Dorset coincided with a trip Tony was making to Canada for a wedding.

I was dreadfully nervous as I drove down to Dorset. Inevitably some painful memories of the events around our parting began to surface but I made a determined effort to block them out. There was no point in us meeting in order to hurl recriminations about the past at each other. I chose instead to take the fact that he had got in touch as a positive sign. He had been a very young man when Duncan was conceived and surely now maturity would have given him a different perspective. Of course, I naturally wondered what had happened to him in the intervening time. I had got a sense that he was on his own and was at a loose moment in his life, but was he separated or divorced and did Duncan have half-brothers and sisters?

I walked into the pub and immediately recognised Simon standing at the bar. I was shocked by his appearance. Everyone changes between their twenties and the midlife years, and I obviously had too, but as well as gaining weight Simon had a reddish flush to his complexion and no longer looked like a man who bothered much about his appearance. Immediately I knew that I was well and truly over him and it was a huge relief to find the hold he'd once had over me was quite broken. There was no longer any attraction there for me.

He bought me a drink and we sat down and began to talk. It was a strange feeling. We had been lovers, now we were pretty well strangers, yet we shared something special; we were the parents of a child. I had brought some pictures of Duncan with me; a few of him growing up and one or two recent ones. I showed Simon the pictures of Duncan as a young man first.

'Don't you think he looks like you?' I asked. Simon glanced at them briefly and said, 'No, not really.' Then he said, 'I've got two children,' and began rummaging in his wallet, finally producing a picture of a boy and girl aged about two and three. 'There,' he said, 'these are my two.' It felt as though he was denying paternity of Duncan all over again. I wanted to say, 'You've got *three* children.'

I felt terribly disappointed and found it impossible to understand how a man could fail to show any interest in his son. Simon seemed oblivious to my reaction and, ordering us both sandwiches, started to ramble on about his own life. He mentioned that he had been married first to a Malaysian woman, and was very keen to stress that she was a famous song writer in her own country. When that marriage hadn't worked out he had formed a relationship with a German woman, the mother of the children whose pictures he carried, although they too were separated. When I inquired where the children were he said they were back in Germany, though it was obvious he was now settled in England. Another set of children growing up without a father, I thought, but said nothing.

I tried to tell him about Duncan's remarkable singing voice but it quickly became obvious that Simon was not in the least bit interested. He only wanted to ask about me and my life. I'd brought the tape Duncan had made at the holiday camp and said, 'You must listen to this, your son is going to be something very special.' Simon took the tape in an absent-minded way but didn't ask for any of the photographs. He started quizzing me again about who I was with and where I lived. I brought things to an end as quickly as I could and drove away feeling despondent and hurt that Simon had no interest in Duncan. But I was also relieved – I had laid a ghost to rest.

Later, in one of my conversations with Duncan, I told him that Simon had been in contact after all these years and that I had been to see him. 'Oh really, what did you think of him?' he asked, and I could tell he was showing a polite interest in something that was part of my life rather than wanting to know for his own reasons. I told him I thought Simon hadn't changed. Duncan had grown up with a very clear impression of my mother's opinion of Simon so he immediately understood what I meant by that and our conversation turned back to the much more fascinating subject of his own life in London.

Duncan had by now responded to various advertisements in *The Stage*. One, which sounded promising, was from someone looking to form a boy band, but although they liked Duncan's voice it never came to anything. Phone calls from Duncan during this time varied from, 'Mum, I'm on the short list!' or 'They say they've got a record label interested!' through to, 'I'm just hoping something will show up.' In those days of course I knew very little about the industry so I just had to listen to Duncan and provide simple encouragement, as he didn't know much then about the way things work either.

Although Duncan was now based in London, still dossing on friends' sofas, he often came back down to Bournemouth for the weekend and he also kept up with lots of his friends from Sidmouth. Then of course there was regular contact with Grandma and Grandpa. Often when he put the phone down to me he would dial my mother's number straight afterwards and chat to her. He filled her in on his news and always wanted to know how they were; he worried about their health a great deal now they were both approaching eighty. For many years after my father's retirement from teaching he had kept busy with plenty of voluntary work. Lately, however, he had slowed down markedly, although my mother was as fit as ever.

I always talked to Duncan about everything in my life and

when, after two years, the stresses of running the guesthouse began to impact on to my relationship with Tony, I shared this with my son. In fact it didn't come as much of a surprise to Duncan. From the outset he had been worried about whether I would adapt to such a very different way of life – a world away from all the things I loved, like the countryside and animals. I hadn't realised that living in a guesthouse, which is essentially a 24-hour, seven-day-a-week business, means you never have any privacy. Our living area was at one end of the house away from the guest rooms but it was cramped and dark. It wasn't a place where Tony and I could unwind and relax. Then there were the endless hours of boredom when I had to be there just in case anyone called, or because I had to be on hand for guests but there wasn't actually anything to do. Tony, I discovered, had an enormous capacity for just sitting and letting the hours slide past, either watching television, reading the paper or pottering about – ideal talents when it came to the patience needed to run a guesthouse. I, on the other hand, liked to be active and all that enforced idleness drove me mad.

In the end the business was destroying our relationship. Tony could see it too and eventually he agreed to sell up and give me my stake back. He had never really liked living in Dorset and when, around this time, he received an invitation to go to Australia for six months he decided to take it. He asked me to go with him but I didn't want to be on the other side of the world for that length of time when Duncan was still so unsettled and my father was getting more frail.

I was wondering what to do next when I bumped into an old girlfriend who was on her own and looking for someone to share a place with. It was a chance to live in the country once more and we had the same ideas about the kind of place we wanted to live in. After some searching we found a fabulous barn conversion to rent on the outskirts of Ferndown, a town near Bournemouth. It had fields surrounding it and some rather ramshackle farm buildings set around an equally dilapidated courtyard area. The owners had built themselves a new house on one side and had two barn conversions made out of one long building split in half. The idea was that they would rent these out as holiday lets and go on to renovate all the other buildings. However, they'd slightly run out of steam and found holiday lets were quite demanding in terms of management, so they were pleased instead to rent the whole place to us on a permanent basis.

Inside it was nicely done with lots of wooden beams and was very roomy with five bedrooms. My friend had a daughter who sometimes came to stay and of course Duncan also came when he could, but the rest of the time we had spare rooms. Our landlords kindly turned a blind eye when we hit on a way of subsidising our rent by letting out spare rooms as overnight accommodation for pilots taking a commercial flying course at the nearby Bournemouth airport.

Of course I brought with me my two Yorkshire terriers, Gordon and Poppy, and it was a relief to be living in a rural setting again. My friend had three cats and, after some initial ruffled fur, all the animals settled down. After moving out of the guesthouse I took a job with an agency providing health care training courses for staff at residential homes. Local authorities now required that staff in these privately run homes had the necessary training and certificates to prove they had attended the courses. I went on a three-day course myself to learn some aspects of presentation, but my nurses training meant I already knew the subject matter, which was about how to move and handle elderly people. This entailed showing them the correct way to lift people from wheelchairs into cars and all sorts of other manoeuvres using specialist equipment, which I carried in my car to use for demonstrations. It was a flexible job and suited me well. The agency would take bookings from homes that had ten members of staff who needed to do the course and would ring me to see if I could manage that appointment. Including travelling time, each course took up about half a day.

I worried a bit about Duncan because I knew his life in London was pretty tough, trying to make ends meet with all sorts of jobs, but I felt his strong personality would always see him through. Around this time we had a lovely family celebration when my younger brother Roddy got married and Duncan and I drove down to the village in Devon where he lived. A huge barn had been transformed for the reception and we had a great day. In the afternoon we sat with our drinks on the grassy banks outside, enjoying the sunshine, and in the evening they held a dance. Duncan and I stayed the night and the following day we made a detour into Sidmouth to see some of our old friends.

Going back prompted lots of memories and, as we were setting off, Duncan began wondering about the fate of our beautiful Main Coon cat, Dakar. When we had left the campsite Dakar wouldn't settle and had begun to stray. He had subsequently been 'adopted' by a local residential home and became their much-loved pet. Duncan was seized by the idea of seeing if Dakar was still there. 'We're really close by, let's just go and pop in,' he persuaded me. We knocked at the door of the home and asked if they still had Dakar. The matron said, 'We certainly do, and it is so fortuitous that you've called today.' It turned out that the home had been taken over and the new owners had instructed the staff to get rid of their three pet cats.

My life has been full of the strangest coincidences but I really felt fate was playing a hand that day. Of course I said immediately we'd love to take him with us but it wasn't to be so easy. Dakar had gone on one of his little walkabouts and though we searched everywhere and called out his name, we couldn't find him. Regretfully we had to abandon the search but I gave the matron my mobile phone number and asked her to get in touch if he turned up. We set off back to Bournemouth but had only been going for twenty minutes when my phone rang and the matron said he'd come back. We immediately turned round to collect him. I was shocked when I saw him. Instead of the silky, fit cat I remembered, he was now so skinny his ribs were showing. I had Poppy and Gordon in the back of the car already and I was a bit worried about managing Dakar as well but there was no way we were going to leave him behind. Duncan drove, while I sat with an extremely tense Dakar, who was petrified of the dogs, perched uneasily on my lap. Once back home I took care to make a special fuss of him and to feed him up but it took a while before he settled, what with two bouncy Yorkshire Terriers and my friend's three cats as well. Even though it was four years since he had been with us I am sure he remembered me and I was so pleased when his old, laid-back personality resurfaced. I had no idea that very soon a set of events was to make me uproot my little menagerie and make another move for very different reasons.

chapter thirteen

The Worst Year of My Life

Some time after my father turned 80 I noticed that he became quieter and rather more withdrawn. He was still interested in everything we had to say when we visited, but there was a definite slowing down, which Duncan commented on too. Up until that point neither of my parents had seemed elderly, either mentally or physically, and I'd imagined, in the way we all delude ourselves, that they'd go on forever. Although my mother was two years older than my father, she suddenly seemed much younger than him and she found his withdrawal slightly frustrating. She was probably lonely too. She was quite a chatterbox, but now my father wasn't communicating with her in the same way. When Duncan and I visited, increasingly it was her we talked to while my father sat in his chair, smoking his pipe, but not taking such an active part in the conversation.

However, they observed the same routines of their daily life and she still looked after him and prepared meals just as she always had. One of the rituals my father enjoyed, apart from his pipe, was a glass of wine in the evening. One night, when he was pouring his glass of wine in the kitchen, he somehow made a mistake. Instead of wine he picked up a bottle of cider vinegar, which did look very much like a wine bottle. He drank two glasses of it without realising his mistake as his taste buds were no longer very sharp. Later that night he began to feel ill and by the following day he was very poorly indeed, with severe sickness and diarrhoea. My mother was terribly worried and called their GP. He said my father had become dehydrated and the sudden loss of fluid was a shock to his body. When my father didn't begin to show any signs of recovery it was arranged for him to be admitted to the local Blandford cottage hospital. They had a room with two beds and it was agreed that my mother could stay with him in the hospital. I went over to give my mother as much support as I could and also to see my father, although my mother warned me that he wasn't responding.

What I saw when I arrived shocked me immensely. The hospital staff had shaved off my father's moustache, presumably to make it easier to insert the two little oxygen tubes that now led through his nostrils to help him breathe. His face looked so naked and defenceless without that familiar moustache and a feeling of hurt and anger overwhelmed me. It seemed just such a personal affront to the proud man I'd known. He was lying on his side with a glazed, unfocused look to his eyes, staring listlessly at the wall. His complexion was a ghostly grey. Tears pricked my eyes and I knew immediately that he wasn't going to get better.

My mother, thankfully, was quite composed. By way of displacement activity she was busying herself with things in the room, seeing to the flowers people had sent and fussing with things she had brought into the hospital with her. Later that day I went to meet Duncan at the station. He had come straight down when I called him to say how ill Grandpa was, and when I took him to the hospital he immediately gave my mother a big hug, something I've always found hard to do. I could see that just having Duncan there was good for her. It was April and he had turned 20 about a week earlier. He told my mother how he'd celebrated with some friends and it was a relief for my mother to hear about life going on outside.

By now my mother had accepted that my father was dying. By the third day she was so tired she needed to lie down and get some sleep on the other bed. I promised I would wake her if there was any change in my father's condition. She had only been asleep for about half an hour when I heard my father's breathing alter, becoming noisier and more laboured. I knew immediately that the pattern of breathing meant he was about to die and had a ridiculous split second of torment about whether to put my head out in the corridor and call for a nurse or wake my mother first. Fortunately I chose my mother and in an instant she flew off the bed and was by his side, holding his hand. Seconds later he was gone.

My mother, for the first time since she was a young woman in her twenties, was on her own, after an incredible 58 years of marriage. She was a woman, very much of her generation, who had put her husband and family first all her life. Indeed, we had *been* her life. In the days following she must have felt so alone but she did what my mother always did – she put on a front and made herself very busy with all the arrangements for the funeral. We had a lovely service for him at the local Catholic church, the same church where I used to follow my parents up the aisle for Communion when I had been embarrassed to be a single mother. My father had been very well liked and the church was filled with friends and acquaintances who had known and admired him. Duncan and I both did readings and sat either side of my mother, together with my brothers Alistair and Roddy and their partners. Afterwards we went back to the house, where I had helped my mother prepare a buffet. We all shared memories of our life with my father over the years and I thought of the many, many times he had been so strong and so loving. His death left a huge gulf in our family, and I could only imagine what my mother must be feeling.

After the funeral I drove over from Bournemouth as often as I could to see her, though my working life had altered, making my free time more restricted. The owner of a large residential home for mentally ill people had been impressed with the way I had run some courses there and had persuaded me to accept a full-time job as manager of the home. It was quite a demanding job with very long hours, but I knew my mother missed having someone to talk to and I wanted to be there for her as much as I could. Duncan was also very concerned about her and worried about her being on her own. She was so important to him and he rang often with little bits of news about his life and to hear about how she was doing.

One beautiful summer day in July I was able to get away from work early and drive over in the afternoon to have tea with her. I found her sitting in the garden reading the *Daily Telegraph* with her elderly dog, Kerri, lying a little distance away under the shade of the trees.

'Hello darling, how lovely to see you,' she said and immediately got up to put the kettle on and make us both tea. She wouldn't hear of me going to make the tea – that old habit of spoiling all the family was still so much part of her make-up. We wanted to have a good chat and it was too hot outside so we moved into the sitting room. She sat in the regular armchair she had always occupied when my father was alive, and I sat opposite on the sofa. She mentioned briefly that she had felt slightly out of sorts the day before but was feeling better today. I had brought her a magazine about dogs because I knew she was debating whether to get another one. My mother had always had a dog and loved to go out walking but now, although she was still fit and active, poor old Kerri was very frail and not up to more than pottering about the garden. We talked about different breeds of dog because, apart from the walking, my mother loved the company of a dog and especially more so now my father was gone.

'Well I think…' she began, after taking a sip of tea from the cup she was holding, but she never finished the sentence. The words degenerated into a slur, like a record player running down, and tea splashed all over her dress as she jerked in spasm and lost control of her arm.

'Mummy!' I screamed in absolute terror. Instinct and emotion took over but still, with a part of my rational mind and my nurse's training, I knew that I was watching her have a stroke. I rang 999 and asked for an ambulance, begging them to be quick. She hadn't lost consciousness but she was very confused. I checked her pulse and kept talking to reassure her. Even though I was a nurse of many years' experience, it's very different when it's your own mother. I was aware that my voice sounded wobbly and strange as I told her it would be all right and that she was safe with me. The ambulance arrived and as the paramedics lifted her very gently on to a stretcher it was obvious that she was totally paralysed down the left side of her body.

I drove behind the ambulance to Dorchester Hospital and on the way called my brothers and Duncan on my mobile. Without hesitation Duncan said he would be on the next train down. Alistair had only to come from Bournemouth and by the time the ambulance arrived he was there at the hospital. Roddy, who drove up from Devon, arrived soon after. As the ambulance staff passed her to the hospital's emergency team my mother was still conscious, giving me hope that if she didn't have a second stroke she would live, although it was obvious the first stroke had been a major one. We could only wait now while doctors evaluated her condition and made her as comfortable as possible. When Duncan arrived in a taxi from the station his face showed that he feared the worst and I was relieved to be able to tell him she was expected to survive.

When someone has a stroke there's very little you can do apart from putting them on medication to thin their blood and reduce the likelihood of a second stroke. You have to rely on the body's natural powers of recovery, so the first step is to let everything in the body settle again after such a major shock to the system. The fact that the stroke was on the left side was significant, because I knew she would still retain her speech. If the stroke is down the right side, speech is always lost or very badly affected. We were able to go and see her when she was transferred to a ward, and my brothers and Duncan were shocked to see the lively, able person we knew suddenly transformed into such a frail creature, with her face lopsided and her left side totally immobilised. It was frightening for all of us. She had a 'nil by mouth' sign at the foot of the bed and was on a drip. One of the major problems after a stroke is the way that swallowing and the actions of the tongue and the mouth are so impaired.

I finally left the hospital late that evening and drove with Duncan back to my place in Ferndown. I was completely exhausted and, after showering and changing my clothes, I flopped down on the sofa while Duncan brought me a cup of tea. It seemed a million years since I had set off on that sunny afternoon to have tea with my mother, yet in just a few hours my world had changed completely. I had rung my work to tell them what had happened and that I was going to need a few days off. Now, as I talked things over with Duncan, I began to think I might have to give them my notice.

My mother stayed in Dorchester Hospital for a week while they assessed her condition. Although they had an intensive stroke programme she wasn't considered a suitable candidate, but the physio team did begin therapy immediately to try to restore the tissues and muscles of her face. This involved holding ice against her skin to stimulate sensation. Other aspects of her care were necessary but horrible for her to endure, like being catheterised. She had always been such a private woman, especially about physical matters, so to protect herself she switched off completely. The stroke had totally robbed her of any sense of balance and that, coupled with the paralysis which rendered her left arm and leg dead, meant she was unable even to sit up in bed unless she was lifted up by two people and propped up carefully. Thankfully she could speak but the affect on her muscles made her voice sound quite different.

I realised that it was going to be a long haul to recovery and knew I had to quit my job. I felt bad not to be able to work any notice but there wasn't really any argument in my mind about who was going to come first. It was a relief when after a week my mother was moved to Blandford cottage hospital, the same place we had all been only three months earlier with my father, as it was so much nearer for me to get to. There she began a proper physiotherapy programme with a couple of sessions a week. I made sure I could attend these whenever possible so I could give her as much encouragement as possible.

She was no longer being fed intravenously but there was a big problem in that she simply wouldn't eat. She had always loved her food but now she didn't want anything. It was a combination of the muscles controlling her mouth and tongue being affected plus a real problem swallowing. In addition the drugs she was taking made her feel nauseous. I would sit for hours trying to coax her to eat tiny mouthfuls, the way you'd feed a child, and Duncan did the same. I scoured the shops for things that would be easy to swallow and bought jars of baby food. She had a plastic beaker, like a child's one, to drink out of and made an effort to take sips of Ribena or cranberry juice.

Sometimes I spent nights at my parents' house when I had stayed late with her at the hospital, instead of going back to my own home in Ferndown. On those occasions I could feel the presence of both my parents so strongly in the house that

I almost expected to see them there. I imagined them as they had been in their seventies, fit and active and delighted to see Duncan and I arrive to share a Sunday lunch with them. Then other memories of them from earlier years would crowd in and make my throat tighten.

One of the saddest decisions I had to make in the first days after my mother's stroke was to have her elderly dog, Kerri, put down. At first I thought of taking her back to my house in Ferndown but when I realised how very infirm she was, only able to take a few steps from house to garden, I knew I couldn't leave her alone to navigate a dog-flap to get in and out, never mind life with two bouncy Yorkshire terriers. My mother had had to go through the agony of having some of her previous dogs put down, and I knew she would agree with my decision, but nevertheless I didn't tell her. I didn't want to speak of anything that would cause extra upset.

My mother began to switch off in a big way, and hated seeing herself in the mirror. I was always wracking my brain to think of things to take in that would arouse some interest from her, little flower arrangements or some other treat. The nurses tended to get her up in a wheelchair and take her, along with some other patients, into the day room where there would be something she wasn't remotely interested in on the television. The real success story was when I hit on the idea of taking my two little Yorkshire terriers into the ward. I asked the staff and they agreed as the therapeutic effect of animals on the elderly and sick is quite well proven. Certainly the visit by those two small dogs proved an excellent boost to my mother's morale. I lifted Poppy up on to the bed beside her and, as she felt the little dog nestle up, my mother's eyes came alive again. She stroked Poppy's silky hair and soft body and I could tell it was soothing and restorative. After that I took both dogs in quite often, but especially Poppy who was very affectionate.

Tony was back from Australia by this time and he and I had become close friends. He was a complete tower of strength for me during this time and I was so grateful for his support. I couldn't really have managed without him. He had known both my parents and was fond of my mother, and he had also become good mates with my brother Alistair, as they both lived in Bournemouth. The two often met up at their favourite pubs for a drink, one of which happened to be right next door to Alistair's house. Once my mother started to improve we were allowed to take her on little walks out of the hospital in her wheelchair. Tony would help me wheel her down the narrow pavement into the town with a blanket over her knees and often Poppy sitting on her lap, which she loved.

This was one time when it was harder for Duncan to buoy me up. He decided from the time when his beloved Grandma went into hospital that he would stay down in Dorset to be by her side, and we staggered our visits so that she had someone with her as much as possible. Often Duncan would go in last thing in the evening to make sure she was tucked up and comfortable for the night. The sight of him always brought a smile to her face, but he had to work to conceal his intense anxiety. In a way that was typical of Duncan he soon got to know all the staff at the hospital and many of the other long-term patients. When he was visiting during the day he would always stop to talk to them in the day room and ask how they were.

As the weeks and then months went by my mother started to make big improvements and my spirits rose. Everything suddenly began to look so much more hopeful. I coaxed and encouraged her along with all her exercises to bring back the use of her left side, telling her, 'Just a little bit more.' Her only wish was to leave the hospital and go home and I did everything in my power to make that happen. I lobbied the consultant, chivvied the physiotherapist and looked into all the ways we could adapt her home to accommodate her limited physical movement, but finally I had to accept it just wasn't practical. My parents' home was a little semi-detached house and didn't even have a room that could easily be turned into a bedroom downstairs. Instead the hospital team said they thought she would be able to move into a nursing home and then, as her improvement continued, that I could even consider a residential home. This was cheering news indeed and I began visiting all the possible ones around Blandford and then took my mother to see some.

As my mother's indomitable spirit began to reassert itself,

however, she went into complete denial about her disabilities. She rejected every one of the homes we saw outright because, in her mind, she was perfectly able to go back to her own home. Unfortunately being with her every day made me the butt of all her frustrations. She got angry and cross with me because, as she saw it, I was not allowing her to go home. 'Just give me a couple of sticks and I'll walk out of here,' she said on more than one occasion, although she still couldn't sit up unaided.

I began to think that maybe I could fulfil her wish in part if she came home to spend one night at her house with me looking after her, but the doctors were adamant she wasn't well enough. I think they were worried that if anything happened to her and she wasn't officially discharged from hospital they would be liable and they refused to take responsibility. I decided to hatch a different plan and take her home secretly. Part of my work running training courses for staff in residential homes had been to teach them how to lift people in and out of wheelchairs and from wheelchairs into cars. I had the necessary piece of equipment, which was just a board, right outside in the back of my car. It would be easier, I thought, with a bit of help, so I naturally enlisted Duncan's aid. Then I told the nurses on the ward we were taking my mother out for a walk in her wheelchair and would be out for quite a while. I had already parked my car in a secluded area at the back of the hospital. We walked briskly around there and stopped by the car. 'We're taking you home for a little visit,' I told my mother. Duncan and I were thrilled when her face lit up with delight. This was definitely one of the times in my mother's life when her rebellious daughter's appetite for breaking the rules won her approval.

Making the manoeuvre with Duncan to help wasn't too difficult. The board fitted from wheelchair to car seat and the side of the wheelchair dropped down so we could lift her on to the board and slide her across into the car. Then we folded up the wheelchair and loaded it into the boot, all the time looking guiltily over our shoulders lest any members of hospital staff who knew us should walk by. It was only a short drive through Blandford and we parked outside the house to perform the same manoeuvre to get her back into her wheelchair. My brother Alistair had been hoping, like me, that she would one day be able to return and in anticipation he had built a ramp over the front door step and another at the back so she could get out into the garden. Although it was now September it was a glorious day and Duncan wheeled her through the house and into the garden while I made tea. We had taken care to give the garden a bit of a tidy up beforehand, though I'm not sure she would have noticed the odd weed. I felt triumphant that I had fulfilled her wish to come back to her house but it was tinged with poignancy. Seeing her sitting in her wheelchair under the tree in the garden my mind flashed back to the day it had all happened. I was very aware of the absence of her dog – she must have been too but she never said anything. I am sure she guessed Kerri had been put down, but spared us both the upset of talking about it.

We stayed about an hour, until I could see she was getting tired. We went through all the procedure in reverse to lift her back into the car and I reassured her we'd be able to do it again. Back in the hospital car park Duncan and I were not so nervous, now that we'd safely accomplished our secret mission, and we wheeled her back to the ward without arousing any suspicion. After that I did it several times more, though it was quite a palaver when I had to manage without Duncan's help, and sometimes she felt so sick I wasn't sure how much enjoyment she got out of it.

It was a month after that first visit that she encountered a serious setback. I was told she had contracted a urinary infection. A course of antibiotics seemed to sort that out, but it was the first of a number of increasing problems as her immune system weakened and she fell prey to all kinds of different infections. She suffered from conjunctivitis, then a bout of gastroenteritis followed, and soon after she got thrush in her mouth. Every time I thought we'd overcome one set of difficulties, something else would go wrong and she'd be back on antibiotics or some other drug regime. Her body was just breaking down and she became so completely low and depressed that she was put on antidepressants.

At this stage she needed a lot of nursing and the staff were very stretched, but I was protective of her and critical when I felt she wasn't getting the level of care she needed. On one occasion they said she had fallen, which I found very hard to understand given that she wasn't able to move around independently at all.

Little things mattered a lot to me. I was terribly upset if I came for a visit and found her nightie needed changing as it was wet or had food down it. Because it was hard for her to manage food and swallowing, her mouth needed to be gently cleaned twice a day. When this hadn't been done I'd hit the roof. I'm sure the staff came to hate me but I didn't care. She was my mother and I wanted her to be made as comfortable as possible.

Gradually, her body became so weakened and she was so utterly miserable that her spirit broke completely. It was agony to see in a woman who had been such a strength for me and for all her family. Duncan and I would get a sick feeling going up those stairs, not knowing what we'd see. She would often have tears streaming down her face and we often came away feeling tearful to see her suffering. She became confused and began to call out in the night for the sister, disturbing the ward. When this happened they would wheel her bed into the day room but soon she was moved into a little side room. There were two beds in the room and I began staying the night, sleeping next to her. She began to become institutionalised, sometimes calling me 'sister' when I responded to her calls in the night, though she still recognised and knew me when she saw my face in the daytime. Duncan and I spent hours with her, going back to the house in Blandford now and again to eat and sort ourselves out. It was a gruelling and emotionally draining time.

The day I discovered that she had been put on morphine

I knew it was the end. I was devastated that the decision had been taken without consulting us. I didn't want her to die, neither did Duncan. I know it was selfish but we didn't want her to leave us. We did everything in our power to keep her alive. Eventually, on the first day of December, she gave up. She wanted to die. Her last words to me were, 'Shoot me, shoot me.'

That day we had left the sister sitting with her while we went back to the house, but almost as soon as we got in the phone rang and they said we should come immediately. We raced back but reached the ward seconds after she had died. Duncan took her hand and then lay on the bed beside her, stroking her hair with tears running down his face. Neither of us could speak. Finally Duncan got up and quietly cut a little lock of her hair to keep. Turning to me he said: 'It's just the two of us now.' I put my arms around him and he bawled his eyes out. His grief was so deep. I tried to keep a grip on my own emotions and be strong for him but I was terribly upset about the way she died. She had struggled with so much pain and died a horrible death.

The funeral service was held at the same Catholic church in Blandford where my father's funeral had taken place, and after the service we followed the coffin to Blandford Cemetery where there was an area set aside for Catholics. It had been decided that she and my father should share a double grave and it was highly emotional, as we stood around for the second time in only eight months, seeing my father's grave dug up again and her coffin lowered on top of his. It was very hard for my brothers to deal with her illness and express the emotions they felt just as profoundly as I did about the loss of our parents. The fact that I lived nearby and wanted to take responsibility meant I had been much more involved and for this reason it fell to me to register her death and make decisions about her tombstone and the inscription. I also had power of attorney and had to sort out the contents of the house and its sale. I found all my father's things were still hanging in the wardrobe alongside my mother's, and packing everything up was a lonely and emotional task. There was also the question of sorting out their papers. That black tin box, which had so fascinated me nearly 40 years ago, was still where they kept everything of significance. There were piles of old letters, photos and documents that took me right back into my childhood. When everything was wound up my brothers, who didn't have children, kindly agreed that we should divide the modest amount that was left four ways to include Duncan. It wasn't much, but I was pleased it gave him some chance of paying off the debts he was running up trying to survive in London.

After the funeral Duncan and I felt a mutual but unspoken need to separate for a while. We had shared the harrowing experience of my mother's decline and death but now we needed space between us. Duncan went through a very tough time for several months after that. The loss of his grandparents was traumatic as they had played such a pivotal role in his early life. I knew what kind of agony he was going through, and I knew he was struggling with the manifold emotions their death had prompted. After my mother's death he said to me, 'Don't go as well, Mummy,' and I knew he had lost someone who had been a core part of his life. I had to step back and let him sort through everything in his own time while I too went through my own course of grieving. I felt mentally and physically exhausted and was crying every day. Duncan and I spoke on the phone of course, but kept a certain emotional distance from each other while we both tried to come to terms with the loss of two people who'd been so central to our lives.

chapter fourteen

My Son, the Local Hero

The first Christmas after my parents' death and the Millennium New Year were times of very mixed emotions. We all gathered together at the barn I was renting in Ferndown – Tony and Duncan as well as my brothers and their partners came over. I think we all felt the need to be together but it was so strange not visiting my parents and I would even catch myself thinking about ringing to talk to them, forgetting for a split second they were no longer there. My mind was laden with images of them and I know Duncan thought about them a great deal, too.

In January 2000 Duncan answered yet another advertisement in *The Stage* magazine. In this instance the individual behind the ad turned out to be a pleasant, well-connected man in his late twenties called Dominic, who wanted to form a band. He had a girlfriend called Melissa who was tall and stunningly attractive with a charming, vivacious manner. This attractive couple lived in Knightsbridge, where Duncan went to meet them. He discovered that Dominic's ambition was to write music and songs, and his dream was to create a group to perform those songs. He clearly had talent but, just as importantly, both he and his girlfriend also seemed to have the wealth to realise that dream and appeared to have the backing of Dominic's parents.

I received jubilant phone calls when Duncan was told they wanted him in the band. Initially the line-up consisted of Duncan, another boy and two girls, but after a while Dominic felt this combination didn't work. He decided to reduce it to a trio – Duncan and the two girls, who were called April and Rita. Soon the group had a name, Tantrum.

Duncan was on a high. Dominic was able to put him on a salary, so for the first time Duncan could manage to rent a flat of his own. He moved to North Finchley with some friends. This was also his first opportunity to have singing lessons. Dominic arranged for them to see a singing coach called Stevie Lang, who used to be a singer herself and had coached Robbie Williams. Duncan got on with her very well and was thrilled when Dominic agreed to pay for regular tuition.

Dominic had the connections and financial power to open up an entirely different world for his embryonic singing trio. This was Duncan's first taste of luxury and he was often on the phone to me saying, 'You'll never guess what Dominic's just done...'

Dominic often invited them round to his beautiful flat in Knightsbridge and would take them out for meals in top restaurants and lavish presents on them. After all the tough times Duncan had been through I was so pleased something was going right at last.

Through the year they got quite a few gigs. Duncan was always telling me this was the Big Chance when a particular talent scout from a record label was coming to hear them. He looked so different in those days, with his hair in a curtain style, but his voice was sounding good and he was benefiting from professional coaching. I went to a couple of concerts and was impressed. I just hoped they would get the deal they wanted.

Although Dominic was a talented songwriter and had the money to finance the group, he didn't have much experience in the business. His creative satisfaction came from writing and composing and I thought it would be good if he had a partner who was equally focused on the industry side. He continued to be incredibly generous to them and at Christmas he gave them each a suitcase of amazing presents – designer clothes and the latest high-tech goodies.

When they didn't meet with any big success, however, Dominic began to wonder if he had the right line-up. He was advised by a record label producer: 'Get rid of both the girls and keep the boy.' Dominic decided to follow his advice. Naturally, by this time all three had become incredibly close, and Duncan was especially friendly with Rita, who was a lovely girl. The news was devastating and Duncan was very upset and angry. I asked him, 'What are you going to do?' In fact he didn't have much of a choice because he had entered into a contract with Dominic, so he hung on for a while but when the contract ended he decided to leave. It was a tough decision based on what had been incredibly useful experience, but ultimately Duncan wasn't convinced it was going to lead anywhere.

He was able to part on good terms with Dominic and to this day Duncan is very good mates with Rita, who has been in several girl bands since and is obviously very talented. Rita's now engaged and when she and Duncan get together they are completely nuts. After his time with Tantrum finished he was right back to square one. To pay the rent on his flat he had to take part-time jobs again and I did what I could, sending him money, although I didn't have very much myself. Although it was disappointing after such high hopes of a breakthrough, Duncan was very realistic. During the time he had worked for Dominic he had made a huge number of contacts, gained a great deal of experience and got settled in London with his own place. He had travelled a long way, both professionally and personally, since his first days as a Dorset lad up in town for the first time.

I sometimes came up to stay a weekend in his flat. Duncan gave me his bedroom while he slept on the sofa. On one such visit we were out in a shopping mall and came across a young guy, about the same age as Duncan, whom he knew vaguely from the audition circuit.

'Hiya mate, how are you?' Duncan said and introduced me. His name was Antony Costa. We stood chatting in the middle of the mall and it turned out they were both at pretty much the same stage, answering ads and trying to get a break. They arranged to meet for a beer. Soon afterwards Duncan told me that they had decided to hook up together. Both boys had good voices and had got to know a few people in the business. Through one of their contacts they got to meet Daniel Glatman who had been in the industry for a few years and was an excellent businessman with some pretty impressive contacts. He had set up his own management company, called Intelligent Music Management, and was on the lookout for talented acts he thought had potential.

Daniel met with Duncan and Antony, liked them and thought he could help. Duncan was open to anything. I had always imagined him going into the West End rather than pop, as he was an all-rounder who could act as well as sing. But as he met all these different people I could see that was not the way he was going to go. It was Daniel who got them an introduction to Hugh Goldsmith, an executive producer and managing director of Innocent Records, one of the three main record labels for Virgin Records UK. Hugh Goldsmith listened to their demo tape and was very pleasant to them. He said he might have an idea in future but that for now they should go away and see what they could do and come back in a few months.

The boys knew they needed to get the numbers right to form a boy band. Duncan had met Lee Ryan on the audition circuit and through him knew his flatmate, Simon, as well. When Antony mentioned he had heard people talking about the singing ability of a boy called Lee, Duncan knew immediately who he meant. They decided to contact Lee and when they told him about their dealings with Daniel Glatman, he came on board. Now there were three of them.

Then Daniel suggested that Duncan, Antony and Lee stage an audition themselves to find two other boys of equal calibre to make up a boy band of five. They had a big response and saw so many singers perform, but no one automatically leapt out. In the end they picked two boys who they thought were the best and went back to ask Hugh Goldsmith if he'd see them perform. They sang a cappella and he seemed pretty impressed, but still there was no definite decision. Instead he kept them dangling. I had phone call after phone call from Duncan saying they'd heard this rumour and that. It was exciting for him but it was also very tense. Would something really happen this time? I lived through every nail-biting cliffhanger with him. It went on for months.

Then one day I got the most exciting phone call of all. 'We're going to get signed!' I was so excited I was shouting with delight, dancing round my kitchen. I had some friends there and they thought I'd gone mad but when they heard they were so excited too. It was a dream come true. Duncan and the boys couldn't believe it; they were finally going to make it.

'You've got to come up to London,' Duncan told me. 'We're meeting the solicitor and all the mums are coming up to celebrate.' I didn't hesitate. I flew round packing an overnight bag and worrying a bit about what to wear. The only smart clothes in my wardrobe suddenly seemed a bit dated. In the end I chose something safe and black and travelled up to London with my head suddenly full of 'what if' fantasies for Duncan and the band. Duncan met me off the train and took me straight to the restaurant, where I was introduced to all the other mums and the boys' solicitor. There was a bit of business chat but mostly it was hugely exciting and a wonderful celebration because, like Duncan, this was what all the other boys and their parents had been hoping and dreaming would happen.

I stayed the night at Duncan's flat and then went back to Dorset. The signing was scheduled for a few days later, but the night before it was due to happen Duncan rang me in a state of shock. He simply couldn't believe it could happen at this late stage, but they had been told that the two boys they'd picked at their audition were to be dropped. Hugh Goldsmith's team had decided at the last minute that the other two didn't fit in, but they were still prepared to go ahead and sign Duncan, Antony and

Lee with the idea that they'd find a fourth.

It was then that Lee came up with the suggestion of Simon, his flatmate. Duncan knew him but none of them had heard him sing so they invited him to audition. They all really liked him and his voice complemented the other three. He was in. It was a pretty amazing break for Simon, but it also proved good for the other three. They finally signed the contract with the record label in the autumn of 2000. Once they were signed they got paid advances against the eventual money the record label hoped they were going to make, so they were all able to drop their part-time jobs. Essentially any signing of unknown talent is always something of a gamble for the record label. They have to be convinced their prospective stars possess the raw talent to warrant the investment they have to make to groom them to professional standards. After that Hugh Goldsmith pretty well decided: 'Right you four, you're going to boot camp.' They needed to be knocked into shape and one of the first steps was singing lessons. Duncan suggested Stevie Lang, who'd become a good friend, and Hugh agreed. She was commissioned to coach Blue and still does to this day.

At first Duncan carried on living in his flat in North Finchley, but then he moved to another flat in the same area because some local friends from his childhood and teenage years were also up in town and wanted to share. One of them was a boy called Paul, whom Duncan had known since he was a little boy in

Blandford and whose mother is a good friend of mine. With that kind of long friendship comes a lot of security and I was just so happy for him. I felt it was what he deserved, especially after he had gone through such a bad time following my mother's death.

I didn't know anything about the music industry so I had no idea what lay ahead. I thought that now they'd been signed they would simply make some records and that hopefully some people would buy those records! I imagined it would be on a small level, certainly at the start. To begin with they did nothing but rehearse and perfect their act. As well as singing lessons they took dance lessons, and then there was the question of what they would wear and how they would look on stage.

Their first single came out the following spring. I thought it would be great if they could get into the top 20, but I was really expecting it to be the top 40 because nobody knew them. Their very first appearance was on *The Big Breakfast*. I watched them alone in my sitting room in Dorset and felt so proud but also worried. They had never played a gig but suddenly there they were on the screen.

For their first recording they were flown to a studio in Norway, which many famous names use. Their very first song was called 'If You Come Back', although it first went under the title of 'I Swear'. We all thought that would be released as their single – it was such a good song. But the recording company decided on another song, recorded at the same time, called 'All Rise'.

Everyone who had heard it was shocked and felt anxious about the decision because 'I Swear' seemed like the safer bet. I never thought for one minute that 'All Rise' would do very well, although it had been written for them by a professional songwriting team.

The week of its release I got a phone call from Duncan on Tuesday. 'Mum, our song is going into the charts at number four! Isn't that amazing? I can't believe it!' I couldn't believe it either. It felt so fantastic. I was dancing round the house wanting to tell the whole world what had happened. From that point the band went steadily upwards. Their album *All Rise* went to number one, as did their next single, 'Too Close'. In the same year that they were launched I sat watching them on TV on *GMTV*, but this time they were a top band. I taped everything. I felt excitement for him and for myself too, I suppose. I was so very, very proud. I used to sit there with a smile on my face just watching him. My only sadness was that my parents weren't there to see this happen. I had very few people to share it with.

The same regrets about his Grandpa and Grandma were also very much in Duncan's mind. Whenever he could he would visit their grave in the Blandford Cemetery and if we went together I would always leave him for a while because he liked to be completely on his own, talking to them both. Visiting their grave became a special source of comfort to Duncan. Even now, whenever he gets any time off, he tries to visit and sit by their gravestone. He'll take shears to trim the grass and flowers to keep it looking special. If he knows I'm going back to Dorset and he can't come he always says, 'Please go to the grave, it must be looking awful, and get some flowers.' Not very long ago I was there on a horrible, cold day and I saw a bit of paper under a stone and wondered what it was. It was a letter Duncan had written to his grandma telling her what had happened to him. It was so sweet. He has so much depth and it's just so sad that they died before they had a chance to witness his success and be just as proud as I am.

After Duncan became well known, which happened very quickly, slipping quietly into a church wasn't always so easy. On one occasion he and I went to a church we'd never visited before and I noticed a few people whispering and pointing. Before the service began Duncan was kneeling in deep prayer, which he always does, and a woman in her fifties actually walked up and tapped him on the shoulder. I couldn't believe she was doing it but she said, 'I'm sorry to disturb you but some girls at the back would like your autograph.' Duncan had to say, 'I'm sorry, not now, I'm praying to my grandma.' I was shocked that someone could be so intrusive in a church.

Alongside my joy at Duncan's success there was a certain sadness as I thought about Simon's absence in his life. I never said anything to Duncan, but secretly I used to wonder if Simon even recognised his own son on the television. I wished Duncan had another parent to be proud of him. My friends said to me, 'I bet Simon gets in touch with you now your son's become successful,' but I wanted Simon to be interested in Duncan because he was his son, not just because he was famous.

Once Blue became a number one band they began to attract a lot of fan mail and needed someone to answer all the letters. Daniel Glatman, their manager, asked Antony's mother, Andrea, and I if we wanted to do it and we said we'd love to. Lee's mother was already very busy with two hairdressing salons she ran in London and Simon's mother had younger children to care for. Andrea was living in Bricket Wood in Hertfordshire and I was living down in Bournemouth, so we had two different PO Box numbers. I set up a little office in my bedroom and soon the postman was bringing me sacks of letters every day. I would read all of them and liaise with Andrea on the phone. We devised a set of pictures and information we could send out to everyone who joined the fan club but some of the letters needed personal answers, and we tried to respond to as many as we could individually. I was still working and had a job in a nursing home, so it was a pretty busy time, but it was fun.

The first time Duncan's new life and celebrity status affected me was when the boys flew out to New York to film a video. I worried a little about the amount of travelling and flying Duncan now had to do, but only in the normal way that you have a twinge about any family or friends flying, especially after you hear a story of a hijack or an air disaster. If I had known what lay ahead of them on that particular trip to New York, however, I would have been absolutely terrified. They flew out on 9 September and they were given a couple of days off to go sightseeing and shopping before shooting the video. The filming was to be done in Brooklyn, using the Twin Towers as a backdrop.

At that time I was working in a nursing home and on 10 September Duncan phoned me at work to say he'd arrived safely and tell me what it was like. Whenever possible during trips like these he still called me every day and sometimes, when there was a lot happening, we spoke more often. Since splitting with Tony there had been no one special in my life, though I had gone out with a few people and the chap I was seeing at the time happened to know New York well. He said I should tell Duncan that if he got a chance he should go up the Twin Towers because the view from the top was spectacular. So when Duncan called on the 10th that's exactly what I said to him. Duncan replied, 'Yeah, OK, that sounds special. I'll try.'

The next day I was at work in the nursing home and I walked past the day room where several of the residents were sitting with the TV on. As I glanced at the screen I saw a series of unbelievable images – what looked like a plane flying directly into the tower. I just could not believe it and stood transfixed as they replayed the scene. Then I heard the commentator confirm that what I had imagined was actually true. I sat down in the nearest chair and froze in horror as the most terrible images began unfolding. Desperate people jumping to their deaths and then the first tower imploding on itself and crashing down taking hundreds of lives. My mouth was dry with fear. Had Duncan followed my advice and gone for a trip to the top of one of the towers? One of the other staff spoke to me and I whispered, 'Oh my God, my son's out there and I've just told him to go up those towers.'

I tried to phone him straight away but of course the whole world was trying to phone their families and loved ones to find out if they were safe. It was impossible to get through. I didn't know what to do to find out what had happened and was frantic with worry. Everybody at the home tried to reassure me with, 'Don't worry, I'm sure he's fine,' as people do, but I had a sick feeling inside. I knew if Duncan was safe he would call me as soon as he could but all afternoon and into the evening there was no word. At the end of my shift, 8pm, I left and I was driving home along the dual carriageway when my phone finally rang. I snatched it up off the passenger seat and pulled into a lay-by. When I heard Duncan's voice I just burst into tears and sat there in the car sobbing with relief and also at the horror of so many lives lost. Duncan just kept saying, 'Mummy, don't worry, we're safe, it's all right.'

When I had calmed down a bit he said, 'I'm sorry I couldn't get through before to let you know. It's just so terrible here.'

Slowly he began to take me through what had happened. They had got up that morning at 5am and were taken to Brooklyn, the famous waterside district of New York alongside the East River where they were due to film. There was a terrific view from there of Brooklyn Bridge with the Twin Towers in the background. There were several big Winnebagos to act as dressing rooms and they all got ready with make-up and the clothes they were to wear for the video. They were beginning to do some test shots for lighting when they heard the first plane coming. Someone looked up and then shouted and they all saw that terrifying moment when the plane disappeared into the building. They couldn't believe what they had seen. Everyone rushed to the water's edge and they were standing there when the second plane came in. They had a completely clear view of that plane sliding horrifically into the building and disappearing from view as neatly as a letter posted into a letter box. Even from where they were they could hear alarms and sirens beginning to go off.

The boys and all the crew were petrified. At that stage no one had any idea whether this was the start of a series of air attacks and, if so, where and how they would strike next. The boys were ordered to get into the minibus and for the four of them and the crew to get the hell out of there. The driver managed to get them away, out on to the highway and they were heading along at about 40 miles an hour when a tyre on the minibus burst. Thankfully they had a driver who was experienced and cool-headed enough to keep control of the bus as it slewed over and he managed to steer it safely into the hard shoulder. They all piled out and were sitting by the side of road when the police came along and helped them get off the highway. They were driven to a hotel in Queensland, another suburb of New York, where they had to stay. From that point Duncan had been trying continually to get through to me but all the lines were jammed with people trying to do the same thing.

I just wanted him home safe with me. I know every family with someone out there felt the same, but nobody could get out. The record company were trying frantically to get them on a plane but of course all flights were halted. I had a series of phone calls with different bits of news one after the other. Duncan rang to say: 'It looks like Virgin are trying to charter a plane to get us home.' But when that wasn't possible it seemed that they might leave with some officials who were flying out, and when that fell through, there was a possibility of a hired jet, but again nothing came of that. Finally, on Saturday morning, Duncan called to say they were going to be able to get out on a British Airways flight. Of course I was petrified about him flying at all now. This was an utterly new form of terrorism and all flights were vulnerable if people were crazy enough to carry out such terrible suicide missions. More than that, I also felt anyone who had any profile at all was more vulnerable as a hostage.

That Sunday it had long been prearranged that the boys were going to do a roadshow in Bournemouth for the local radio station. Of course with Duncan being a Dorset lad with a lot of connections in the area it was quite a big deal, and lots of people were planning to go, including many of Duncan's and my friends. After what had happened, and the tightness of the timing with their plane only flying in overnight and arriving on Sunday morning, I thought Duncan wasn't going to do be able to do it. I wished he could though and Duncan wanted to as well. There was a feeling that the only way we could fight such senseless terrorism was to try to carry on with life. Playing his first live performance in his home town since being part of a number one band meant a lot to him.

That morning I tuned in the radio and heard the station apologising because they had had to cancel the show after the boys had been caught up in the New York terror attack. Then half an hour later I heard the DJ say that amazingly the show was back on and they were going to play after all! The boys were landing at Heathrow on that Sunday morning and driving straight down to Bournemouth, heading first of all for my house to use as somewhere to change for the gig.

Because this was everyone's first chance to see them safe and sound since those horrific TV scenes in New York, Antony's parents, Mike and Andrea, drove down and Lee's mum came as well. Simon's family lived in Manchester so it was harder for them to get there. We were all waiting anxiously for the band to arrive, and then suddenly my place was full of the boys and their gear was strewn all across the floor. They had Johnny, their tour manager, with them and he was sorting out clothes and chivvying them up because they had so little time. Everyone was hugging them, we were just so relieved to have them back, and I dashed round making cups of tea. It was my first taste of seeing them all together as a band in action and it was quite something. They had to rush, taking turns to get in the shower and then struggling into their outfits for the show. I felt so proud as well as relieved and excited.

The boys all looked absolutely shattered but they were such heroes of the day for making that huge effort to get there. On the radio the DJs were saying they had so much respect for the boys. After what they had been through they had still come down to fulfil the booking, without even stopping off to drop their things home. Together with all the other parents I went to the roadshow and that was my first taste of the impact of fame. We arrived with the boys and of course lots of photographers and local TV were there. I naturally hung back to let them get good pictures of the boys. I was totally taken aback when they caught sight of me and began swarming round, saying, 'You're Duncan's mum, aren't you? What was it like? Tell us how you felt.' As Duncan was the local boy and I was all the family he had there I became the focus of their interest. There were all these questions and they took a photograph of me with the four boys to put in the papers. Watching them perform after the agony of those terrible scenes from New York was so emotional. All us mums held hands and cried, with pride and relief.

chapter fifteen

Fame, Fans and Five-star Fun

Duncan's life seemed to be gathering pace with an almost frightening speed. After the Twin Towers incident the band went straight on to record their next single. I couldn't believe the hectic schedules they had to fulfil. They were constantly rehearsing, touring or recording and so much of their time was taken up with travelling. On tour the boys were told what their schedule was and had no control over it. It usually started at 8am with a radio interview for an hour, and after that it was full on throughout the day with no stops until they got back to their hotel late at night. Of course, it was all hugely enjoyable for four fit young men, but I had the kind of worries that are typical of a parent. They always seemed to be getting on and off planes and there were very few free days to sort out their lives or unwind. The pressure was intense.

Duncan's flat-sharing days were over and he wanted to buy a

house. In the midst of such a frantic life he needed a base and he talked to me about moving from Dorset and coming up to London. I was very pleased. With both my parents dead there was nothing to keep me in Dorset any more and lots of factors made such a move feel right. Duncan had entered into a new world of showbiz and he wanted to share the experience with me. Of course, I was delighted he felt that way as I wanted to share it all with him, too. The fact that I was young when Duncan was born meant that now I was still interested in going out and having an exciting time, enjoying many of the same things he did. In addition we were both on our own without a committed partner – although of course that could have changed at any point, especially in Duncan's case – but in my case it meant I was a free agent. The fact that I was a single parent and he was an only child also made us especially close. Finally, there was the running of the fan club to consider. It was getting increasingly hard for Andrea and I to manage working long-distance from our homes.

So I uprooted everything, including my two dogs and Dakar the cat. At first we rented a detached, furnished house in Bricket Wood near Andrea's home in Hertfordshire. I had some anxieties about moving, as I didn't know anybody in the area apart from Andrea and her family, but they were very hospitable and welcoming to me. Duncan was only occasionally around and it was good to have an immediate focus with the fan club, which needed to be put on an official footing. Andrea and I found a tiny little office with Velux windows and, though it was a bit cramped with two of us and often other people calling in as well, it was in a nice complex of offices and it suited us.

We both worked hard at developing the club, going to the office every day from 10am to 5pm. At first we paid ourselves £50 per week and then £100 per week, which were pretty sparse wages but we were doing it because we wanted to, not for the money. Naturally we got a lot of letters from young girls but, much to our surprise, we also received quite a number of letters from older women in their thirties or forties. It was very weird reading letters from married women saying that when they made love to their husbands all they thought about was Duncan. I couldn't believe it and wondered what on earth was happening, but I also thought it was quite funny. It takes a bit of adjusting to suddenly see your child as a fantasy pin-up for married women!

I started to go with Andrea and her husband Mike to shows where Blue were playing, at venues like the London Arena and Earls Court. We had VIP passes to go backstage and I loved seeing the boys perform, meeting lots of glamorous people and, of course, enjoying the odd glass of champagne which we seemed to be offered at almost every event we went to. The first major event I went to was the aftershow party for the BRITs, in February 2002, where Blue won Best British Newcomer. I also went along sometimes to various TV studios when they were performing or taking part as guests. It was a whole new world to me. I'd never been inside a TV studio in my life, never mind having a behind-the-scenes view of how it all worked. It was fascinating seeing the camera and sound crews with their miles of cables and leads and watching how the floor manager worked.

The boys in Blue were big celebrities now and I began to meet other famous people at events and parties. At first I was really nervous and couldn't imagine anyone would be at all interested in talking to me. I used to wonder what on earth I could find to say. I was just Duncan's mum. Then I began to understand that, in fact, being Duncan's mum gave me a status, a reason to be part of it all, and that these people were very happy to meet me and talk to me because of that. Duncan was also very keen to introduce me to everyone. He'd always say, 'My mum's here, come and meet my mum.'

Duncan, together with the other boys in Blue, took part in the TV show *An Audience with Donny Osmond* and sang with him. After the show Duncan took me backstage and I met Donny and his wife, who were so charming and friendly. When we found a house to buy, Duncan invited lots of the people he'd worked with to our house-warming party and it was there I met Danni Behr for the first time. She was great fun and very friendly. After we'd met a few times, she was due to have all four boys on her TV show and she asked me to help her play a little trick on Duncan. They were answering phone-in questions from fans and then Danni suddenly said, 'Duncan, I've got someone on the phone for you... Oh, it's your mother. Hello, is that Mummy-Duncan?' Duncan's face looked absolutely horrified for a moment because he obviously thought I'd taken leave of my senses. 'What are you calling about, Mummy-Duncan?' Danni asked, and I said I was ringing because I wanted to tell Duncan he'd forgotten to shave that morning. At the time he had a little wispy, goatee beard. All the other three boys were in hysterics and Duncan, who was beginning to suspect he was the victim of a set-up but still wasn't quite sure, took the phone and said, 'Mother, stop embarrassing me!'

Another guest at our party was Dale Winton, who Duncan had got to know, and Dale invited me to come to his book launch soon afterwards where I met Barbara Windsor. Duncan also asked Cilla Black to our house-warming after working with her when he went on a special celebrity edition of *Blind Date*. Sadly she couldn't come but she sent me flowers and a lovely message saying: 'So sorry I can't be with you today but I am filming a new show called *Sing with a Star*. I bet you are so proud of your lovely son Duncan, I know I am. Lots of love, Cilla.' All my life I'd been very sociable and loved to fill my house with people, and now I mixed my long-standing friends with celebrities. Just as Duncan enjoyed sharing his new life with me, so I got great pleasure sharing it with all my friends, too.

One of Duncan's friends I especially liked was Tara Palmer-Tomkinson. She and Duncan have now formed a production company. Tara is very kind and completely honest in what she says, which I admire because I speak the truth too. She talked to me about her cocaine addiction and how supportive her parents were. She can be completely crackers with a huge capacity for fun, so she's great to be with. On one occasion the three of us went to a teddy-bear factory where you can dress the teddy bears, tape your voice and stick the message in the back of the bear. She bought one for Duncan that says, 'Hello, Duncan' in Tara's voice.

When Blue performed at Wembley as a culmination of their UK tour I went every night and took different friends. One very pleasant result of finding my real mother, Audrey, is the friendship I now have with my cousins – Amanda, who lives with her family in Birmingham and Cath, who lives in Dartford, Kent. They both came to see the show at Wembley and Amanda's teenage children loved discovering they had such a cool relative in Duncan. My half-brother Paul, Audrey's son, couldn't come down to Wembley but Duncan got him tickets to see it in Manchester and come backstage afterwards.

Seeing Blue perform isn't exactly to Audrey's taste, and her health isn't tremendously good, but she's very proud of Duncan. She's been down to visit us in Hertfordshire and Duncan has completely accepted the new side of his family that emerged as a result of my voyage of discovery. When he was a teenager and my parents were still alive, he experienced a sense of divided loyalty but now he is very fond of Audrey. Although fame has naturally boosted his ego he is still the same very caring, sensitive person.

He took great pleasure, for example, in fixing up for my brother Alistair and his partner, Monica, to go on a special holiday.

My new glamorous social life definitely put my wardrobe under a certain amount of pressure! Luckily Duncan loves treating me and I chose a couple of dresses from a shop in Hampstead for my birthday, one of which I wore to the BRITs 2002 aftershow party. Duncan didn't come with me but paid for them over the phone with his credit card, although on other occasions he's brought me back things from trips that he chose himself. He's always had the most terrific natural taste, ever since he was a young boy, and he's got a real eye for things I'll like, whether it's jewellery, perfume or clothes. He often rings me from airports when he's about to buy something and wants to check if the size is right. I had a brown fringed suede jacket and he bought me a pair of beautiful fringed suede boots that matched exactly. I trust his judgement totally and if I'm going out, but in doubt about an outfit, I'll always ask his opinion.

At first this role reversal regarding money felt a bit uncomfortable. I'd supported him for so many years and suddenly, as he was the one with the chequebook we'd switched round. Over time, however, we achieved a new balance. I tried to advise him about money and warned him to be careful that people didn't rip him off, but he's got a financial adviser. Certainly I loved the other little treats that crept into my life as a result of having a pop star son. I started having my nails done every fortnight, which I never did before, and now I'm quite addicted. If I'm going somewhere special I also have a stylist called Karen, who's become a friend, who comes to my house and does my hair. Duncan's always coming back with beauty products that companies have sent, wanting celebrities to test them. He'll say, 'Try this, it's supposed to be really good for your eyes.' The boys have to keep very fit and have a trainer to take them through workouts at a health centre. I sometimes go there with a girlfriend for a swim and to enjoy the jacuzzi and sauna.

The one treat I absolutely love, which has become part of my life now, is to have a car and a driver whenever I go out. Duncan is fiercely protective – he insists that if I go out anywhere in London I take one of the record company's cars and always tells the driver to stay with me all evening. A beautiful Mercedes with blacked-out windows turns up and I just hop in, usually with a girlfriend, and we're delivered door to door. When we arrive and the driver gets out to open our door, everyone looks to see what famous person it might be, and it's just me! But I love feeling so special – like a queen.

The other side of celebrity life, which I am just as pleased about, is the chance to do something worthwhile for charity, especially those causes which are not particularly fashionable and find it harder to attract support. It was through a friend that I got involved in a charity event to raise money and support for young people with Crohn's Disease. Crohn's is an inflammatory bowel disease that can affect all ages, including children and teenagers, and can be hard to diagnose because its symptoms are similar to

Irritable Bowel Syndrome and another type of inflammatory bowel disease called Ulcerative Colitis. I took part in a sponsored ten-mile walk in Hyde Park called 'Walk for Crohn's' and Duncan and all the boys in Blue signed up to give £10 a mile. Best of all, Duncan was able to come along and put in a quick appearance at the beginning to say a few words and sign autographs. His schedule was incredibly tight and at one point it didn't look like he could do it, so I was very proud he made such an effort.

Just before Christmas 2002 we went on holiday to Florida with some friends. I don't know whether it was experiencing so much change in his life or the loss of his grandparents but Duncan suddenly said, 'I want to meet Simon.' This was the first time in his life he had ever mentioned his father and I was quite unprepared. He'd grown up always knowing what had happened regarding Simon and he had totally accepted it and never shown the slightest interest. Duncan said he just wanted to see what Simon looked like and added, 'Before he dies or something,' so I suppose the loss of my parents had played a part. I didn't say anything. I had an immediately protective feeling for Duncan, remembering Simon's lack of interest. I couldn't bear Duncan to be hurt or rejected. Over a certain period he mentioned it a couple more times, then he got incredible busy with the band and the subject was dropped.

Early in 2003 the band were doing a tour of the Far East and the record company said that if I, or any of the other parents, wanted to go we could. I knew Blue were big in Japan but I was amazed when there were over 1000 girls to meet them at the airport, all going absolutely ballistic. We were all pretty shattered after the flight and it was over an hour's drive to the hotel, so the boys didn't pause there too long. Lots of fans followed our cars and when we got to the hotel there were masses more waiting. The boys were exhausted but they signed autographs and posed for pictures. It's not unusual for them when they're touring to come off a flight and only an hour later be performing or beginning a load of interviews, but on this particular tour they had the rest of the day off so we all went to sleep.

Every day there were hordes of fans hanging around the hotel but the Japanese fans are so respectful and so courteous. They were older than the very young fans we often see in England, many in their twenties. As well as being charming they were also very generous and wanted to give the boys presents, which they had brought with them all neatly wrapped up. When they found out I was Duncan's mum I became the focus of their attention, too. They wanted to take my photograph and talk to me. They told me how much they loved Duncan and said, 'Thank you for giving us Duncan, we love you, you're so lovely, we love your son.'

On my return I thought again about Duncan and Simon. My one wish that I had held inside me all my life was for Duncan to meet his father. I was never going to suggest it as I wanted it to come from Duncan himself. In the end it finally came out in an angry way, not a soft way. That might have been because all Duncan knew about Simon he'd picked up from my mother's attitude, which was, 'We don't talk about that creature, he left your mother and that's it.' I decided that whatever my fears about Simon's lack of interest, if Duncan wanted to get in touch I should help him. But the truth was I had no idea where Simon might be now. Our meeting had been four years ago and I'd got the impression his visit to the West Country might have been a temporary stop-off. I went on the Internet and did a search using Google. Two Roscoes came up in the Swanage area. I just had a hunch about one address and I called the number. A woman's voice answered. When I said I was trying to contact a Simon Roscoe she asked who I was. I said it was a personal matter and she said, 'He's not here but we can probably get a message to him.' I gave my mobile number and within an hour I got a call from him, by which time I was in a pub with Andrea Costa. He said, 'It's Simon, how are you?'

'I'm fine,' I replied. 'The reason I'm phoning is because your son wants to meet you.' Silence then, 'OK.'

I said, 'He's famous now, you know.'

'What are you talking about?'

'He's in a pop band.'

'How would I know that?'

'He's in Blue.' When Simon heard that he became quite emotional and burst into tears.

'You've really blown me away on this one,' was all he managed to say. He's a guy who really likes to be in control of his emotions and doesn't want to reveal too much about himself, so he must have been totally taken by surprise to react in that way. However, next minute I could hear the self-obsessed side coming through when he said, 'Well, I've been quite famous in my life, too.' I found it unbelievable that he could immediately feel competitive and try to turn the conversation towards himself.

'I haven't called to talk about you, Duncan wants to meet you,' I said and told him we'd speak later. He rang me back a couple of hours later when I was back at home and we had a chat, but now he didn't seem particularly interested in Duncan or Blue. I told him about their achievements but he didn't react. He seemed more interested in me than in Duncan. How was I? What had I been doing? He went on to tell me he was a writer and had had books published. Now, he said, he was working on a film to be made in Croatia and it was going to be massive. He said that the two of us should meet again.

Simon and I had several more conversations after that and it so happened that I was going to Sidmouth a week later to stay with my girlfriend from school days, Bindi, and another friend, Janet. I mentioned this to Simon and he suggested I come to meet him in Torquay, where he was living. I wasn't sure I wanted to, but on an impulse I rang him on the day of the journey and said I would meet him after all with my girlfriends in a pub.

When we arrived at the pub, which was in Babbacome, a

suburb of Torquay, Simon was the only person in the pub. He had changed in the four years since we'd last met, and looked more thickset. He was very distressed because his elderly dog, Freddie, was very ill and said he almost didn't come. Loving animals was something we'd had in common and Simon almost seemed to be one of those people who prefer animals to people. When he went up to the bar to get a drink, Blue's hit with Sir Elton John, 'Sorry Seems To Be The Hardest Word', came on. It seemed incredibly appropriate but when I said, 'Listen, can you believe this?' he just said, 'Yes, I can'. He didn't react emotionally. I don't think 'sorry' is a word Simon even has in his vocabulary. Certainly I knew the song would never make him think about running away from Duncan and me years ago. He doesn't think he has anything to apologise for.

Bindi and Janet asked him why he had not been interested, all these years, in knowing about his own son. Simon said it was because he had been sent away to boarding school, aged six. He blamed everything on his childhood. He talked in a rather rambling, disjointed way, going off at a tangent all the time, which he never used to do before, so it was hard to follow the thread of everything he was saying. He talked about his son and daughter from the relationship he'd had with a German woman. The children were now aged about 11 and 13 and lived with their mother, Maya, who had since married and had a third child, near Baden-Baden in Germany. Bindi asked if he saw them much and

Simon said his daughter, the eldest, scarcely spoke any English, so it was hard to communicate. When Bindi asked, 'Why didn't you learn German?' he replied, 'Well, we won the war.'

It was hard to get through to him. When my friends tried to make him realise how huge Blue were and that Duncan couldn't even walk down the street without someone asking for his autograph, Simon said he knew all about fame. He writes under the name of Steve James as Stephen and James are his second names, which is a strange coincidence as Duncan's stage name is Duncan James. Now Simon talked about how everybody knew the name Steve James in the Far East. He went on to tell me about how he and Maya had gone out to Spain where they'd run a restaurant. It was another disjointed, hard-to-follow conversation and, once again, Simon didn't seem interested in Duncan, only in me. I thought about how his son had turned out to be a much bigger man than his father.

Simon asked me if we would all go back to his house with him because he wanted me to see his dog, knowing how much I love animals. He was living in a rented house in Torquay and had obviously been going through some old papers. He showed me a newspaper cutting – a picture of his wedding to the Malaysian woman – and said, 'I should never have married her.' I saw he had lots of old passports on a desk and I picked up one from around the time we had been together. Seeing the passport picture of him as a young man brought back lots of memories. The resemblance to

Duncan was striking. I had not one picture of Simon to give Duncan if he ever asked, so, without saying why, I asked if I could have it.

It had been a very odd day and I was glad my friends had been there to stop it feeling completely unreal. After that Simon rang quite frequently. I had said Duncan might want to make contact with his half brother and sister, as Blue play in Munich quite regularly, and Simon gave me their mother's phone number. Simon also said how much he had enjoyed our meeting and that he thought I looked lovely. He wanted to meet again. Then he went so far as to say, 'I think you and I should get together.' When I asked why he said, 'I love you, I've always loved you.' 'I'm sorry,' I told him, 'you're 25 years too late.'

chapter sixteen

Private Life, Public Face.

Just as there turned out to be similarities I never had expected between the life of my real mother, Audrey, and myself, in that we were both young women who gave birth alone, so there is an echo of my experiences in Duncan's life. I had found a whole new family after tracking down Audrey and now after I had met up with Simon again, Duncan discovered he had a half brother and sister.

Simon went through a stage of ringing me frequently after our meeting in Torquay and on one occasion Duncan happened to be in the house. I knew Simon would do nothing to instigate a meeting with Duncan. He is a man who avoids any possible hint of trouble or confrontation, and although that kind of reaction was the last thing on Duncan's mind I guessed Simon would be afraid of recrimination. Duncan, for his part, was reserved about taking the first steps without some kind of positive sign from Simon. How to ever get them together? On an impulse I said to Simon,

'Duncan's here now, you can speak to him,' and before he had a chance to say no I called Duncan and passed the phone to him, saying, 'It's Simon, he wants to say hello.'

Duncan looked shocked but after a second's hesitation he took the phone. I went out of the room then and the conversation lasted barely a minute, with Duncan saying, 'Hello mate, how are you?' and just hearing awkward sounds from Simon at the other end. I thought how typical it was that Duncan had to make the running and take the adult role in their first encounter. Afterwards Duncan didn't say much about Simon but he mentioned again that he would like to meet his half brother and sister, who lived in Germany.

I gave Duncan the phone number of their mother, Maya, and soon afterwards an opportunity arose as Blue were playing in Germany and one of the gigs was to be in Munich. Duncan rang Maya to introduce himself and set up a meeting. She had been pre-warned by Simon that Duncan might call and she knew all about his background and the success of Blue, who were equally big in Germany. By now Maya had a new partner, with whom she'd had a baby, but she was delighted to drive to Munich and bring her older two to the concert. Duncan's schedule, as always, was incredibly tight and the only time he could manage to squeeze a little space was after doing a photo shoot in a studio. It wasn't ideal but it was better than meeting backstage with all the usual entourage around. I was both nervous and excited on Duncan's behalf and I know he felt the same. 'I'll ring you, Mum,' he promised, 'and tell you how it goes.'

True to his word, he was actually so eager to tell me all about the encounter that he went off into the loo to ring and give me an immediate report while Maya and the children were getting their things together. Duncan was so animated on the phone, I knew it had gone well, and he said, 'They are both so lovely.' That's just typical of the spontaneous way Duncan expresses himself and shares experiences. Of course when he got home he sat down and filled me in on all the details. This is how he described their meeting:

'I spoke to Maya a couple of times on the phone and knew that my half sister was called Tara and was 11, and my half brother, Julian, was 14. I felt nervous about meeting them. It was a strange thing to think we shared a father and yet, for me, this was a person I'd never known or met so we couldn't talk about the one thing we had in common. Tara and Julian know their grandparents on Simon's side, who are also my grandparents, of course, but again, I've never met them. For the children, at their age, the biggest thing about the meeting was probably just the simple fact that they have a relative who is a pop star. It was lovely to learn that they are fans of Blue and excited about that aspect of my life, but at the same time

fame does sometimes get in the way. I couldn't help but be aware that I would probably find it easier to get to know them if I weren't successful.

My first impressions – which have stayed the same now that we've met several times more – were that they were sweet-looking children who were very polite with lovely manners. I was immediately struck by certain ways Julian resembled me at that age, he's got my eyes, and because he speaks pretty good English it was easier to communicate with him. Tara doesn't speak English so that made it harder, but to set them both, and Maya, at their ease I took the lead and asked them lots of questions about music and the show just to make conversation. All my experience as a kid of working at the campsite and then the jobs I had as a Redcoat at a holiday camp make it easy for me to help people feel relaxed.

When I was growing up I sometimes used to think I'd like an older sister and a younger brother, not in any kind of serious sense but in the fantasy way kids have of imagining an ideal family. I never imagined I'd come by a half brother and sister in this way though. There's nothing heavy about our relationship, they're just kids, but I like knowing them and we've met up a couple more times since because I'm often playing in Germany.

Maya talked to me about my father, which was a bit difficult, but really just confirmed the impressions I'd already got. I hope it's a friendship that will continue because the age gap between Tara, Julian and I will narrow as they grow up.'

Since then Maya and I have exchanged emails and talked on the phone and this summer Maya is going to bring the children over to stay with me in Hertfordshire. The dates will coincide with a tour Blue are doing so I can take them to a concert. I'm really pleased for Duncan because although he's got loads of friends, there's something different about knowing who your relatives are. For me it will be a very strange experience. I am going to meet a woman with whom I have one thing in common, but know very little about, and I'm going to meet Duncan's half brother and sister who are not in any way related to me.

I left the whole question of whether Duncan would take steps to meet Simon up to him. I felt I had done all I could and now it was a very personal decision for him to make in his own time. Meanwhile, establishing a new direction in my own life was becoming a priority again. Andrea and I had long since handed the fan club on to professional managers, as it had simply become too vast, and Duncan had less need for me to provide a base. He had bought a beautiful flat not too far away in Hertfordshire, though since he'd left most of his absolutely vast wardrobe cluttering two rooms of my house, he was still a pretty frequent visitor.

Duncan had thought about buying a place in southern Spain and I had entertained the idea of spending part of the year out there, possibly even moving there permanently. We arranged to visit over a long weekend, together with Daniel, Blue's manager who is also a friend of Duncan's, and one of my friends, to look at some properties south of Marbella. As we walked through the airport terminal at Malaga, Duncan switched on his mobile phone and it rang immediately. I could tell straight away from his troubled expression that what he was hearing was not good news.

'I don't believe it – what does it say?'

By this time we had all stopped as Duncan stood still and listened intently. When he finally hung up he turned to me with an angry expression and said fiercely, 'Simon's given an interview to the *Daily Mirror*.' I was completely stunned. My anxiety about Simon had always centred on his total lack of interest in his son. Although Duncan and Daniel were immediately of the opinion that Simon had approached the paper offering to sell his story, I found it impossible to believe. Could a man who had no interest in his son suddenly decide to exploit that connection for money? That evening Simon rang me, sounding annoyed, and gave me a rambling story about how his mother had been hounded by the press and had given them his number. It was an unlikely tale, given that the name

Roscoe doesn't feature on Duncan's birth certificate, and one that I still cannot believe to this day.

Once we reached our hotel I called a friend who read the story over the phone to me. My confusion turned to anger. It certainly appeared to be an interview given with Simon's co-operation but from my perspective it was full of inaccuracies. Simon claimed to have spoken to Duncan several times on the phone, and that their conversations had been short and acrimonious, which has never appeared to be the case. He also said I had sent him tickets to a Blue concert at Powderham Castle near Exeter – a total fabrication. Needless to say there was no mention of his appalling behaviour concerning Duncan's birth. Instead, he implied his relationship with me had been a casual fling and he hadn't known I was pregnant until we split up. That was terribly hurtful, and so too were the revelations of certain highly personal details, like the fact that I was adopted. Duncan was equally angry and upset. At first I was pretty much the focus of blame as his first reaction was that it would have been better never to have contacted Simon. Once we'd all calmed down, however, the thing that really hit us both was that Simon seemed to prefer talking to the media than spending time getting to know his son. I am sure for Duncan it must have revived memories of the views his grandma used to express when Simon's name was mentioned. Sadly it was an act that seemed to jeopardise, if not entirely close the door, on any kind of future relationship.

Fortunately the momentum in Duncan's life was so great that he seemed reasonably able to put the whole matter to one side on our return to England. The band was going from strength to strength and success continued to bring a raft of new experiences for them and for me. One of the most memorable was when Blue was invited to perform at the Queen's Golden Jubilee rock and pop concert, Party at the Palace, in the gardens of Buckingham Palace in 2002, and I received an invitation, along with the other parents. It was tremendously exciting to be going through those famous gates at the front of the Palace on such a special occasion. We arrived in the late afternoon and queued through various state rooms to pass tight security checks, finally emerging at the back of the palace on to steps leading down to the gardens. Everyone was given an individual picnic box and we were able to wander all around the stunning setting. It was the most tranquil scene with majestic trees and wonderful beds of shrubs and flowers set around a large lake. It was hard to believe we were in the heart of London. There had been a lot of jokes beforehand about what staging a pop concert would do to the Queen's garden if it rained but, in the event, it was a beautiful summer day.

When it was finally time to take our seats I was shown to a raised area with a great view of the two stages and a clear view of the Royal Box. When I saw Princes Charles, William, Harry and nearly all the other members of the Royal family take their seats

I knew the concert was about to start. From the opening chords of the national anthem, played by Queen guitarist Brian May on the rooftops of the palace, it was an absolutely magical evening. Later the Queen and Prince Philip arrived and took their places in the Royal Box. As the sun disappeared and the temperature dropped my only regret was that I hadn't worn something warmer as I'd dressed for a summer day. I couldn't help noticing that all the female members of the Royal family were given blankets to ward off the chill!

The evening was a non-stop line-up of the biggest names in the world of pop and rock, from stars like Sir Paul McCartney, Eric Clapton, Dame Shirley Bassey, Aretha Franklin and Sir Cliff Richard to younger acts like The Corrs, Will Young, S Club 7 and Atomic Kitten. There was lots of unusual mixing and matching of different generations of performers, so S Club 7 performed with Sir Cliff Richard and Blue did two numbers with Tom Jones. I know Duncan thought it was fantastic to perform with such a legendary name and I read later that Tom Jones said part of the great atmosphere was due to these collaborations between so many entertainers who wouldn't ordinarily perform together.

After the concert the Queen, with Prince Philip, went out into the massed crowds in the Mall to light the National Beacon, which signalled the start of a spectacular finale of fireworks. Inside the palace grounds there was a big screen enabling us to see all this as well as the fantastic light projections on the façade of

Buckingham Palace. All the performers stayed for a big aftershow party. When I was home I got a series of excited phone calls from Duncan: 'Mum, I've been just been chatting with William,' or 'You'll never guess – I had a really long conversation with Princess Anne.' He was just as excited to meet so many huge names in pop as well, like Sir Cliff Richard.

Another first for Duncan in 2002 was presenting the Elle Style Awards on TV. The event, which is a really glamorous affair, was staged at the Natural History Museum. Duncan gave me a ticket to share a table with the rest of Blue and their friends and family as the band, including Duncan, were presenting one of the awards. It was a real all-star evening and Duncan was backstage interviewing the winners of different categories, including 'Most Stylish' actor, actress, music star, designer, model and so on. It was a new experience for him but I didn't feel nervous on his behalf because I have such confidence in his personality and know just being his natural self will see him through. He has the ability to set everyone at their ease and when I watched him later on video I could see his genuine interest in people coming through. After the awards ceremony he was free to join us again and we all went through into another area of the museum, which was fantastically done out like a jungle, to have drinks and socialise. As always Duncan was keen to introduce me to all the people he knew or had just been interviewing and it was a really fun evening.

For Christmas 2002 Duncan and I went away on a cruise,

which we often do because since my parents died I find that time of year quite difficult, and in the New Year Duncan had so many air miles he treated me to a shopping trip to New York on Concorde, which was just the most fantastic surprise. On our return the pop industry was beginning to gear up to the big event of the year, the BRITs, which once more coincided with my birthday. I was thrilled when I heard Blue were nominated again, this time competing on a shortlist for the award of Best Pop Act against Enrique Iglesias, Gareth Gates, Pink and Will Young. I really wanted to go to the awards ceremony itself, but there was no way that Duncan or any of the boys could get complimentary tickets as access is very strictly limited. The only way they could bring any guests was to buy tickets, which cost over £500 each, so in the end they got together and each bought their mums a ticket. I was so excited to be able to attend and Duncan bought me a lovely dress to wear, which I chose from a boutique in town.

I thought they'd done brilliantly to get nominated a second year running, after winning Best British Newcomers the year before, and I tried not to build too much expectation as the competition was very stiff. The BRITs is an event where no one has any idea at all who the winners will be until the announcement is made; there are no leaks or tips beforehand. When Blue were named as the winners we all went absolutely mad. I just wanted to grab Duncan and hug him but the boys were sitting down near the front and we were sitting much further back and higher up, separated from them by a sort of gangway and a barrier. I said to Lee's mum, Sheila, 'I'm going to go down to see them.' 'You can't!' she said. But when she saw I was going anyway, she said, 'If you're going, I'm coming,' and followed me down. When I got to the barrier I shouted out to Duncan, who turned and then walked straight over without any hesitation and gave me a big hug. Lee saw his mum was there and so he followed and, by this time, Simon's and Antony's mums had come down too. Soon all of us were there hugging the boys in total euphoria!

Inevitably any members of a pop band think about the future and how their careers will diversify. For Duncan, acting, presenting and composing are as interesting and rewarding as performing and when he was approached about another, more demanding, television presenting job he saw it as a challenge and a great opportunity. Channel Five wanted him to join forces with Denise Van Outen and a number of others to present Party in the Park, a massive day-long concert staged by Capital Radio in London's Hyde Park in aid of The Prince's Trust. Blue were due to be one of the main acts there and at first I thought it might be difficult for Duncan to be both presenter and performer. However, when he discovered that Blue were to be one of the last acts at 7.30pm, Duncan was able to commit to presenting during the day. It was still an ambitious plan. The show was going out live, with all the possible glitches that might entail, and Duncan also had to use 'talkback' for the first time, which means having an earpiece so that the producers can communicate during airtime with presenters, telling them when to wind things up, spin something out or that the schedule has unexpectedly changed. While the audience in Hyde Park would be kept entertained with live music for seven hours, the TV viewers at home would also see members of the various acts take part in games and phone-ins with the public. Duncan was presented with a stack of paper a mile high detailing the running order, schedules and various cues that he had to learn. He rang me on the morning of the concert to say, 'I haven't slept all night, I'm just so nervous!'

I had passes to the hospitality area, which included a free bar and a section with a good view of the stage, and I arranged to take three girlfriends with me. A little of Duncan's apprehension rubbed off on me after his call, but I didn't have any serious worries because I just knew his personality would win through. It was one of the hottest days of the year and when I saw the size of the crowd I could only imagine what he would feel like up on stage in front of so many people. The 100,000-strong crowd, which literally stretched as far as you could see across Hyde Park, was the largest he had ever faced. In the event his days as a rep at a holiday camp turned out to be quite a good background to draw on because everyone was there to have a good time with a definite holiday feeling in the air. With Denise Van Outen acting as umpire one of the things Duncan had to do was compete with Capital Radio's Kate Lawler, who won Big

Brother in 2002 and went on to become a DJ and morning TV presenter, as to which half of the crowd they could get to shout loudest. The idea was that whichever presenter lost, whether it was Duncan or Kate, would have to take his or her top off. Surprise, surprise – in a largely female audience Kate's side won and Duncan had to forfeit his T-shirt to the accompaniment of much screaming and yelling, which he later told me he felt a bit embarrassed about.

I was briefly able to see him in action backstage in a little garden area Channel Five had created for the competitions and phone-ins. I could tell there was a lot to handle, callers they were expecting to speak to got cut off unexpectedly, or they were suddenly required to speed up a section because the next band or singer was about to start on stage. In the middle of all this I was aware of an extra buzz of activity from the security men as Prince Charles arrived. Later Duncan was in the line-up introduced to him backstage, in his case for the second time.

Duncan finished an eight-hour stint presenting and then had a short break to get himself ready to return to the stage with Blue. When the boys appeared towards the end of an amazing day of live music and the opening notes of 'One Love' sounded, the huge crowd went absolutely mad. I squeezed my way towards the front – even in the VIP section it was a terrific crush as people craned to get a good view – and it struck me what an incredible journey both Duncan and I had made.

A day or so later Duncan called round and took me through some parts of the show I hadn't been able to see on video, fast-forwarding and then stopping to laugh and explain how he'd been put on the spot at some point or other by the director saying one thing in his ear while he had to carry on doing another thing to camera. I loved hearing all the behind-the-scenes gossip because during the show, of course, I hadn't been able to speak to him at all. We got to the end and then Duncan switched off the video and we both fell silent. I was thinking how I wished my parents had still been alive. I so wanted the two people who'd loved Duncan as much as I did to share my pride in his success.

My own upbringing had been unusual, in as far as I was adopted, but I could never have hoped for more loving parents than the ones I had. Duncan's childhood, in turn, had also marked him out. He had been one of very few children at school with a single parent. Mine was the first generation where more women who had babies outside marriage kept their children, often with the support of loving grandparents, instead of giving them up for adoption. While my parents were alive they had been a source of such strength and comfort for both of us. Since their death I had often wondered if I could be enough for Duncan on my own. I searched around for something to say that didn't betray my slightly melancholy mood, but instead it was Duncan who broke the silence and it was as though his mind had mirrored mine. His words however, were unexpected:

'Don't worry, Mum,' he said, giving my hand a squeeze. 'I'm sure Grandpa and Grandma somehow know what's happening. It's not just the two of us.'